AW WITH WORDS

Young Writers' 16th Annual Poetry Competition

It is feeling and force of imagination that make us eloquent.

How can I not dream while writing? The blank page gives a right to dream.

Essex Vol II
Edited by Annabel Cook

First published in Great Britain in 2007 by:
Young Writers
Remus House
Coltsfoot Drive
Peterborough
PE2 9JX
Telephone: 01733 890066
Website: www.youngwriters.co.uk

All Rights Reserved

© Copyright Contributors 2007

SB ISBN 978-1 84602 978 3

Foreword

This year, the Young Writers' *Away With Words* competition proudly presents a showcase of the best poetic talent selected from thousands of up-and-coming writers nationwide.

Young Writers was established in 1991 to promote the reading and writing of poetry within schools and to the young of today. Our books nurture and inspire confidence in the ability of young writers and provide a snapshot of poems written in schools and at home by budding poets of the future.

The thought, effort, imagination and hard work put into each poem impressed us all and the task of selecting poems was a difficult but nevertheless enjoyable experience.

We hope you are as pleased as we are with the final selection and that you and your family continue to be entertained with *Away With Words Essex Vol II* for many years to come.

Contents

All Saints RC Comprehensive School
Ayoola Adedeji (13) — 1

Chafford Hundred Campus
Madeleine Day (14) — 2
Kirsty Howe (13) — 3
Holly Tsang-Holmes (14) — 4
Jake Newell (13) — 5

Chalvedon School & Sixth Form College
Richard O'Connor (12) — 6
Ryan Fuller (12) — 7
Shannon Leeds (12) — 8
Kyna Mott (12) — 9
David Davies (12) — 10
Lidia Farrington (11) — 11
Kieran Howlett (11) — 12
Jean-Pierre Nsinga (12) — 13
Reece Hughes (12) — 14
Amie Harris (12) — 15
Steven Buck (12) — 16
Maddison Couzens (12) — 17
Josephine Kaguathi (12) — 18
Josie Hand (11) — 19
Gabriella Villa (12) — 20
Emma Greenland (11) — 21
Shannon Healy (11) — 22
Chantelle Daniel (11) — 23
Jade Scally (13) — 24
Nicola Anderson (13) — 25
Michelle Banks (15) — 26
Jasmin Pearson (15) — 27
Cara Carter (15) — 28
Jake Blackford (13) — 29
Sian Montague (12) — 30
Darren Gardner (12) — 31
David Foster (12) — 32
Becky Plumb (12) — 33

Jake Langton (12)	34
Haydn Gale (11)	35
Alex Nye (12)	36
Ellie-Rose Hearn (11)	37
George Kaylor (12)	38
Sam Smith (11)	39
Jessica Norris (11)	40
Amy Wheeler (11)	41
Lucy Jones	42
Chel-c Farmer (13)	43
Rebecca Hewins (12)	44
Chantelle Ralph (13)	45
Emily Snoding (12)	46
Charlie Wallin (12)	47
Kita Clark (13)	48
Sean Pittom (12)	49
Dogan Omer	50
Sammy-Jo Brazil	51
Chloe Boyle (12)	52
Millie Levey (11)	53
Abi Pullan (12)	54
Cameron Greaves (12)	55
Jack Biggs (13)	56
Luke Winter (12)	57
Zack Johnson (13)	58
Dale Basham (13)	59
Samantha Rogers (12)	60
Jessica Steward (12)	61
Natalie Bohea (13)	62
Lorna Warren (14)	63
Jade Alden (13)	64
James Busby (12)	65
Laranina Gillanders (12)	66
Annie Harvey (13)	67
Mitchell Stocker (12)	68
Alaina Smith (13)	69
Alexandra Belcher (12)	70
Tanya Bolding (13)	71
Chelsey Fox (13)	72
Rebecca Skerritt (12)	73
Kayleigh Bradon (12)	74
Jordan Cosburn (12)	75

Josh Bailey (13)	76
Jay Stone (13)	77
Chloe West (12)	78
Tara Pacey (12)	79
Josh Turner-Mason	80
Georgina Bailey	81
Jacqueline Barnard	82
Emily Gunn	83
China Benton	84
Elizabeth Cater (12)	85
Alfie Smith (13)	86
Shane Reynders (13)	87
Luke Jones (13)	88
Luke Baker (13)	89
Dominic Niyazi (11)	90
Paige Goodgame (11)	91
Gillian Abbott (11)	92
Charlotte Cater (11)	93
Dominic Villiers (12)	94
Kelly Plumpton (12)	95
Ryan Fredericks (12)	96
Daniel Niall (12)	97
Billy Cash (12)	98
Hannah Neale (13)	99
Jade Gutteridge (12)	100
Kelly Vince (13)	101
Jade Smith (13)	102
Jodie Padmore (12)	103
Annam Mehreen (12)	104
Jennifer Frimpong (12)	105
Charlotte Bettle (12)	106

King's Wood School

Camie Broomfield (16)	107
Toni Wicks (16)	108
Jack Cassie (16)	109
April Bailey (13)	110
Caroline Murray (13)	111
Lewis Thwaites (13)	112
Kelsey Bridges (13)	113
Lauren Stripling (14)	114

Martin Cunningham (Davis) (13)	115
Sam Harding (13)	116
Francesca Morley (13)	117
Samantha Davies (16)	118
Harriett Ray (13)	120
Charlie Edwards (13)	121
Katie Marsh (16)	122
Louise Reddington (16)	123
Lucy Cadby (15)	124
Georgina Pope (15)	126
Precious Sibanda (15)	127

St Bernard's High School, Westcliff-on-Sea

Morgan Power (11)	128
Sophie Wizik (12)	129
Vittoria Murphy (11)	130
Jasmine Davison-Holmes (11)	131
Shannon Wood (12)	132
Chloe Guest (13)	133
Chloë Wells (12)	134
Claudia Devlin (13)	135
Mary Imbush (12)	136
Melanie Horton (14)	137
Emma Nee	138
Sarah Arnold	139

Sawyers Hall College

Sophie Bell (12)	140
Lucy Webber	142
Holly Nott (12)	143
Lily Sawyer (13)	144
Jack Foulger (13)	145
Bambo Banjo (12)	146
Jake Kimberley (12)	147
Michael Watts (12)	148
Jamie Kingston (12)	149
Joe Ward (12)	150
Charlie Parker (13)	151
Gabby Wallace (12)	152
Fern Royffe (13)	153
Sam Sparks (13)	154

Kieran O'Shea (12)	155
Ryan Bishop-Olejnik	156
Keeleigh Hogan (13)	157
Lily Bolden (12)	158
Elle Jopson (12)	159

The Gateway Academy

Amy Richards (13)	160
Craig Madle (13)	161
Hayley Bannister (13)	162

The Sydney Russell School

Jessica Ingando (13)	163
Vesela Maslenishka (14)	164
Esther Osarfo-Mensah (14)	165
Manpreet Kaur Hunjan (12)	166
Akyaa Boakye-Ansah (13)	167
Gurleen Kaur Hunjan (14)	168

Woodbridge High School

Kyle Powell (15)	169
Natalie Williams (14)	170
Sam Everitt (14)	171
Georgia Green (14)	172
Amritpal Malhi (14)	173
Nicola Thompson (13)	174
Danni Bicette (11)	175
Luke Jones-Saunders (13)	176
Lauren-Amber Morgan (13)	177
Hayley Shannon (12)	178
Alistair Bolt (12)	179
Jasmin Johnson (12)	180
Charlie Wade (13)	181

The Poems

Silence Before The War

The battlefield stays silent,
As the rider puts on his faithful silver armour,
The eerie silence is petrifying,
The mystical rider hooks his ruby sword,
The majestic beast spreads its wings.

The battlefield stays silent,
The majestic beast is fitted its silver armour,
The scene of fear is unnerving,
As the beast's sapphire eyes shine like two great stars,
It shoots tongues of bright blue flames down at the earth.

The battlefield stays silent,
As the rider's men are handed their weapons,
The eyes of their enemy are hallowing,
They stand ready but not all of them will make it,
They look for guidance from their rider,
The rider and dragon unite and soar.
The battle has now begun.

Ayoola Adedeji (13)
All Saints RC Comprehensive School

Innocent Moonlight

Moonlight innocently shines,
A bit of hope in these weary times,
Casting shadows upon the dead,
Lighting fields of bloody red.

Taking energy where there's none,
A fading hope of the rising sun,
Reaching down to those departed,
Almost kind and warm-hearted.

A last sad sight for a man to see,
A world from which we are free.

Madeleine Day (14)
Chafford Hundred Campus

My Love For You

My love for you
is like the sky
with hopes that soar
and dreams that fly.
It's like a never-ending ocean
and everlasting deep emotion,
it has the tenderness of spring
the charm and warmth
and laughter brings.

Kirsty Howe (13)
Chafford Hundred Campus

Ignored Love

She lays and thinks of him at night,
While other girls are in a fight,
Her every dream is just for him,
Until he comes, her world is dim.

Her perfect world is them together,
Not just for now, but until forever,
She won't tell him her perfect thought
It's just a dream, but she got caught.

She sees him every day,
But it's not clear as she backs away,
Watching him walking by,
Doesn't say a word, she feels too shy.

Her true feelings are now hidden,
But their love is not forbidden,
She needs to wake up and open her eyes,
He likes her a lot, she just doesn't realise.

Her emotions are deep, but her heart is not whole,
She finds it too hard to capture his soul,
She thinks he ignores her, but he tries to catch her eye,
He knows that he loves her, that's one thing he can't deny.

In time they realise how they both feel,
This love is too strong, the scar will never heal,
Over the years they end up as a couple,
Their love is real and very subtle.

The moral is as clear as can be,
They are happy and in love, can't you see?
Together now, that's how it should be,
Don't ignore love, it can end in tragedy.

Holly Tsang-Holmes (14)
Chafford Hundred Campus

Scuba Diving In Australia

We climbed onto the scuba boat,
Slowly rocking on the smooth, clear blue waves,
We put on our scuba gear,
I walked to the side,
Total silence, as I plunged into the water
The instructor made my suit less buoyant.

As I went under, I couldn't hear nothing
But the water moved as I did
Blue water as far as the eye can see
As I went deeper, coral and fish form.

I was at the bottom
Small fish darting around me
Of all colours
Swimming in groups
They looked me in the eye
And just swam away.

I had to go then
My suit made me buoyant
We emerged from the water
I thought to myself . . .
Wow!

Jake Newell (13)
Chafford Hundred Campus

Gangster's Paradise

I have a gun and a knife
But by the risk of losing my life,
It gains me respect
It gives me something to protect.

So I've killed someone
What's done is done,
I had to run
I didn't think it was fun.

I had a knife fight
I knew it wasn't right,
Now my long life is gone
I got stabbed by the don.

Carrying knives is a death sentence
My death was no coincidence,
Respect your life
Not a knife.

Richard O'Connor (12)
Chalvedon School & Sixth Form College

Dragons

D angerous and fiery,
R oaring whilst burning fields to pieces,
A mazing flames come roaring out,
G one in a flash,
O nly once it had finished,
N obody can slay the foul beast,
S o it stays soaring in the sky.

Ryan Fuller (12)
Chalvedon School & Sixth Form College

Fantastic Fantasy Flies Away

Imagine fairies in the wood,
Imagine what you dream,
Imagine that evil witch's cat,
Imagine dwarves making cream,
Just imagine that.

Fairies are fantasy,
Dreams are like fantasy.

I'm dreaming of nature,
I'm dreaming of spells,
I'm dreaming of catching those naughty elves.

Away in the night,
I'm dreaming away,
By fairies and fantasy,
All by me.

Shannon Leeds (12)
Chalvedon School & Sixth Form College

Fluttering Flower

Flower, flower in the night,
Like the sun it is so bright,
Delicate and soft like talcum powder,
This is my little garden flower,

Swaying in the autumn breeze,
Though it can do whatever it please,
In winter it is all alone,
But in spring it can go home.

Kyna Mott (12)
Chalvedon School & Sixth Form College

Football Fever

Kick the ball like it's on fire,
Commentator gets it wrong cos he's a liar.
Run down the field and nick the ball.
Slide tackles them so they'll fall.
Get the ball in the net.
We will win I bet.

David Davies (12)
Chalvedon School & Sixth Form College

Babies

Babies cry, babies lie.
Babies eat and drink tonight.
Babies speak and scream a lot
Babies are tiny little dots.
Babies may be ill
Babies can even feel a little chill.
Babies at birth may go blue
Babies at birth may look at you.
Forget all of those things
Think about the babies that die
Think of those parents that have to say *goodbye*.

Lidia Farrington (11)
Chalvedon School & Sixth Form College

What Shape Should It Be?

A
Triangle
Is too pointy
And sharp. It
Would make my
Words sour not sweet.

A square is
Like a box
That will trap
My words.

A rectangle
Drags on
And on.

An
Arrow
No!
It
Will
Draw your eyes
From the
Words

Perhaps
A hexagon
Or maybe not
Because of
Boredom.

A
Circle
Shows ever-
Lasting words
That go on an
On and on
And on.

Kieran Howlett (11)
Chalvedon School & Sixth Form College

Christmas

Christmas, the day of God.
Christmas, presents and happiness.
Christmas, buying presents for someone that we love.
Christmas, a day of snow, laughter and surprise.

Christmas, a day of celebration that we have in the heart.
Christmas, a day of emotion, happiness, families and chocolate.
Christmas, when Santa Claus comes with his Christmas presents
and puts them beneath your Christmas tree.

Christmas, when the world is celebrating a happy and
merry Christmas on the 25th December
but they forget that when they are having great fun
some people are not,
some people are outside begging for money or food.

Why does Santa Claus give presents to us?
Why not the poor?
Christmas, a good day and a sad day.

Jean-Pierre Nsinga (12)
Chalvedon School & Sixth Form College

Mushroom, A Menace To Society

M onstrous mushroom just sitting there
U nder the tree, near the well
S uch words can't describe its ugliness
H owever it has a slight beauty
R adiant in only one way
O ver its horrid exterior
O ver its hard outer shell
M ushrooms, tiny babies just sitting there,
   sitting there near the well.

Reece Hughes (12)
Chalvedon School & Sixth Form College

Friendship

Friends are like glue, they stick together
No matter what, they'll stick by your side
Friendship is meant to last forever
No matter what the weather

When you're cold or when you're hot
Your friendship should never stop
When you cry or when you smile
Arguments should come once in a while

A real friend has love in the heart
Until your friendship has to part
Now she's moved the feeling has gone
You will always be my number one.

Amie Harris (12)
Chalvedon School & Sixth Form College

Chocolate

C is for chocolate chip cookie goodness
H is for honey-flavoured caramel
O is for obviously chocolately
C is for caramel-covered bar
O is for oh so chocolately
L is for lovely milk chocolate and a caramel filling
A is for a lot of chocolate
T is for tremendous chocolate
E is for erosion of chocolately goodness.

Steven Buck (12)
Chalvedon School & Sixth Form College

My Chihuahua

I have a pet chihuahua, yes I said chihuahua,
Her eyes are big, she likes to dig,
I love my pet chihuahua.

My chihuahua is just the best,
She is never a pest.
She loves me so, I'll never let her go,
I love my cute chihuahua.

Her fur is short and ginger,
She can be such a whinger,
She would walk all day and drag me the wrong way,
I love my sweet chihuahua.

Maddison Couzens (12)
Chalvedon School & Sixth Form College

My Apple

A n apple so crunchy, an apple so sweet.
P eeling an apple.
P lease give me an apple so I can taste the sweet.
L oads and loads of apples so tender and sweet.
E veryone happy to get a fair taste.

Josephine Kaguathi (12)
Chalvedon School & Sixth Form College

Bullying Is A Crime

I hate bullying, I think it's cruel,
Bullying is as cruel as a cheetah,
Why do people do it? It makes life hell,
Some people commit suicide but they shouldn't, they should tell,
What is the point in jumping in front of a train?
When your whole life's ahead of you, don't be afraid,
Just stand up high and live your lives
Because soon there will be a sign, *'no bullies allowed!'*

Josie Hand (11)
Chalvedon School & Sixth Form College

My Family

One day my family went weird.
Everyone was shouting and getting cross.
Never get involved.
But it is always about one thing, *me!*
Everyone in my family kisses and cuddles me.
It is too bad, but again it is always about one thing, *me!*
My mum and dad fight like lions when they get mad.
But I really miss the fun times when we all got along.
But it is always about one thing, *me!*
My family are really weird
Now this is my family and don't forget
Sometimes it is all about *me!*
But did I forget to tell you, my family is a little weird.

Gabriella Villa (12)
Chalvedon School & Sixth Form College

My Family

M y family are caring and kind.
Y esterday I went round my cousins Tia's and Chrissie's.
F amilies are kind and caring, I love everyone in my family.
A nd my mum and dad and my sister and me all live
  in the same house but my brothers live on their own,
  I'm an auntie.
M y mum is the best ever, my dad is the greatest ever
  and my sister is just plain annoying.
I love my family more then anything in the world.
L ove is a caring thing, deep down in your heart
Y ou love me and I will love you.

Emma Greenland (11)
Chalvedon School & Sixth Form College

Dogs

Dogs are cute
Some wear little suits
They have four legs
And two ears
Some are big
Some are small
But they are all so cute in their little way
Some say dogs bark
Some say dogs don't
Some say dogs are like humans
Some don't
Dogs are smart
Dogs are dumb
But dogs are all different kinds.

Shannon Healy (11)
Chalvedon School & Sixth Form College

Coward Bullies

Bullying her, bullying him
Bullying is as horrible as Brussels sprouts.
He bullies her and she bullies him,
Don't you have anything better to do?
Just because they have different features,
Just go and tell the teachers.
Bullying makes people lash out
And teachers don't know what it's about.
Bullying can also make people commit suicide
And parents would be upset that they have died.
Don't bully, be friends or you'll regret it,
Until your life ends!

Chantelle Daniel (11)
Chalvedon School & Sixth Form College

Respect

Love is a flower
You are my flower
So treat it like you want to be treated
You are as sweet as a flower
I would know because you are my flower.

Jade Scally (13)
Chalvedon School & Sixth Form College

My Nan

Soft as a flower,
Never too sour.
Loved to cuddle me,
My heart was locked and only she had the key.

My sweet nan,
God bless you.
My love for you hasn't died,
My love for you is so true.

I cry myself to sleep,
My love is yours to keep.
You were my guardian angel,
I love you.

My sweet nan,
God bless you.
My love for you hasn't died,
My love for you is so true.
I love you.

You were my nutty nan,
You didn't care that you didn't have a man.
I miss you my dear nanny,
So, so much, please come home.
You were like a queen on her throne
Oh . . . *I love you.*

Nicola Anderson (13)
Chalvedon School & Sixth Form College

Why Do It?

Wherever I go you're always puffing
You just don't care whether people are suffering
Puff, puff, puff every day and every night
I just can't seem to get the smoke out of my sight

You tell me don't do it, but you do it yourself
You know damn well it's affecting your health
So, please can you stop, just give it a try
I'll be so happy as time goes on by
It don't take a genius to work out it's wrong
And plus when you stop, it won't take you so long
So just give it up now, I'll beg on my knees
It's all I am asking, so please Mummy please
It would make me so happy
It would make me so proud
For you to get rid of that grey smoky cloud
You would be so much healthier
And happy to know
No more yellow teeth
And no more smelly clothes

So just pack it in now
And give it a rest
Thank you for listening
Mum you're the best!

Michelle Banks (15)
Chalvedon School & Sixth Form College

Now You Are Gone

Now that you are gone, I realise how much I care,
And now that you're gone, I wish that I was there.
To help you through the good days and through the bad,
Every time I had to say bye, I became so sad.
Sad because I had to go, sad because you were in pain,
Even on the sunniest of days, it felt like rain.
Because rain is gloomy, rain is sad,
Sad is the emotion I felt, along with feeling bad.
Bad for leaving you each night alone in your bed,
But now you're in a peaceful place, because now you are dead.
Each and every day, we will have you in our hearts,
Each and every day, we'll never feel apart.
Because you watch us from above, you watch us as we pray,
You watch us from morning till night, when we pray.

Jasmin Pearson (15)
Chalvedon School & Sixth Form College

The Victim

I wasn't popular
I had no friends
I had no confidence
And felt nobody cared

People would laugh
When I was beaten to the ground
Grateful it wasn't them
I was the victim

I couldn't speak out
I was too scared
I let it happen
My family never knew

That's when I decided
Nobody would miss me
But now I know
It's not true

What I did was stupid
I should have thought it through
But it's too late now
I've been put to rest.

Cara Carter (15)
Chalvedon School & Sixth Form College

Football Is The Best

Sport is the best
It comes from north, east, south and west
Some might like baseball
But the best sport is obviously football

Football is shocking or even insane
20 teams in a league, most of the players feel pain
West Ham, Man U and Tottenham, they all play the game

Arsenal are the best, you can just tell
Man U are the team that live in Hell.

Jake Blackford (13)
Chalvedon School & Sixth Form College

Bullies

Today is another day at school
when people pick on you, just to make themselves look big.
They came up to me today
and knocked the books out of my hands.

I never stand up for myself and I should.
I said, 'Why are you picking on me,
would you like it, if I picked on you?'

Stop being a bully, no one likes bullies.
Now she has never spoken to me since.
School is much better now no one picks on me,
it's not very nice.

Sian Montague (12)
Chalvedon School & Sixth Form College

Life At War

Bang! go grenades
Boom! go bombs
'Help me,' shout people, crying for help
Wee! go planes over the gloomy sky
Kzkzkz goes the radio
This is life at war
Woo! go the air sirens
'Argh!' go people, running for their lives
This life in the war
'Thank you God for stopping this mess,'
Go people saying and praying.

Darren Gardner (12)
Chalvedon School & Sixth Form College

Red

Red is the colour of love
After eating some grub.
I love my mum
Even when we used to play scrum.
I love my dad
Even when he bought me a cat.
Red, red, red, red
Is easily spread.

David Foster (12)
Chalvedon School & Sixth Form College

Friends

Always on the phone talking to my friend.
Why I run up and down the stairs.
Singing, 'Happy New Year'.
Playing on the laptop with my friend.
Like all day and all night.
Having a sleepover, up all night long.
Talking about this and that, like all that.
My friends are the best.
Things in the world.
Up all night, can't wake up in the morning.
Why my mum shouts at us.
So we decide to get up.
Everyone needs a friend or friends.

Becky Plumb (12)
Chalvedon School & Sixth Form College

Red Is Just The Best

Red is my favourite colour
Red is just the best
Red is the colour of a football team
Red is the colour of a bean
Red is the colour of blood-red
Red is the colour when people are dead
Red is the colour of burnt down trees
Red is the colour of a bite from fleas
Red is the colour of the light
That comes out of the end of the laser gun
But when you play with the gun it is so much fun
Red is the colour of red heat
Red is my favourite colour
Red is just the best.

Jake Langton (12)
Chalvedon School & Sixth Form College

Colours

Bright
Light
Ugly
Equal
And
Red is the colour of anger
Evil
Death
And
Grass
Remaining there for
Eternity
Even when blackened
Never-ending
And
Orange is the colour of an orange
Round
And
Nice
Generous amount of
Energy.

Haydn Gale (11)
Chalvedon School & Sixth Form College

Trench Warfare - Remember The Soldiers That Died In The War

The smell of a rubber gas mask strikes fear into the wearer.
The sound of biplanes passing above the sky
The wet and muddy soldiers saying their prayers
For the order over the top.
A boy in front of me who was fourteen strapped a Bible to his chest
The thunder of guns going off into the distance,
The numbing sound of the Vickers mg burning off rounds,
Then the sergeant called, 'Fix bayonets,'
The boy in front put in a new clip,
The sergeant took out his whistle and blew,
And then the order came, he shouted, 'Over the top'
Fear racing through my mind, I jumped into a fox hole,
And then the boy was running into the fox hole where I was,
He stopped, blood fell from his head, he fell to the ground.

Alex Nye (12)
Chalvedon School & Sixth Form College

My Christmas Day

On Christmas Day I went outside to play,
But I felt guilty because it was my sister's birthday,
I love the snow,
Oh no! My sister's on her Poe,
I opened my gifts,
I love what I got,
I got my mum a lovely pot,
Shh, my little sister has gone to sleep,
Try not to make a peep
And that's what I did this year,
Adults go out and grab a beer!

Ellie-Rose Hearn (11)
Chalvedon School & Sixth Form College

Red

Red is the colour at night
Red is the brilliant colour of West Ham's kit
Red is the colour of the fire engines
Red is the colour of blood
Red is the colour of poppies that grow in the field
Red is the colour of stop at the traffic lights
Red is the colour of anger
Red is the colour of danger
Red is a colour
Red is the colour of your heart
Red is some people's best colour
A red cross is the colour of the English flag
Red is the colour of your lungs
Red is one of the colours of fire.

George Kaylor (12)
Chalvedon School & Sixth Form College

Blue

Blue is the colour of a smooth salty sea,
Blue is the sky rising up and up from me.
Blue is a raging wave destroying and drowning,
Blue is the feeling you get when you feel cold,
Blue is the colour of old bread mould.
Blue is the opposite to the blood colour red,
Blue is the feeling when people are dead.
Blue is a nightmare screaming out to you,
Blue is the colour when you play round with voodoo.
Blue is the colour of an ice-cold room,
Blue is the sound of a sonic boom.
Blue is the colour of my bedroom walls,
Blue is the sound when a dog calls.
Blue is my colour and red I dréad,
Blue is the end, the end of the end.

Sam Smith (11)
Chalvedon School & Sixth Form College

Orange

Orange is the colour for a beautiful sunset.
Orange is the colour for an orange.
Orange is the colour for a pumpkin.
Orange is a colour for the power.
Orange is the colour for a goldfish.
Orange is the colour for a clownfish.
Orange is the colour for a carrot.
Orange is the colour for fire.
Orange is the colour for a Californian poppy.
Orange is the colour for lava.
Orange is the colour for orange juice.
Orange is the colour for an Irish setter dog.
Orange is the colour for an oriole bird.
Orange is the colour for a victory.
Orange is the colour for a piece of pumpkin pie.
Orange is the colour for a yam.

Jessica Norris (11)
Chalvedon School & Sixth Form College

Blue

Blue is the colour of the sky on a winter's day.
Blue is the colour of sad faces.
Blue is the colour of fresh water from a glass.
Blue is the colour of my favourite socks.
Blue is the colour of a beautiful animal named the dolphin.
Blue is the colour of the eyeshadow on my eyes.
Blue is the colour of the border in the classroom.
Blue is the colour of a nice boy's eyes.
Blue is the colour of my chair.

Amy Wheeler (11)
Chalvedon School & Sixth Form College

My Poem About My Friends

I'm happy when I see my friends,
Always laughing until it ends.
I'm happy when we go shopping,
I also like it when my friends pop in.
I hate it when we fight a lot,
I feel like I'm on the spot
But then I love it when we sort it out,
It brings us closer without a doubt.
I love having them sleep over,
When we are all crashed out on the sofa.
We are always texting, day and night,
I hate it when my friends are out of sight.
My friends mean the world to me,
They're the best friends that friends can be.

Lucy Jones
Chalvedon School & Sixth Form College

I Shall Never Forget You

When my brother said he was moving to Australia
I just laughed, I thought it was a joke,
But on Christmas Day he said his goodbyes,
A lot of water filled my eyes.
A few hours later he took to the sky,
From that day and forever I shall never forget,
The day that he was holding me, the day that we met,
Brother and sister love, I shall never forget,
If I shall die today or live forever,
I shall tell no lie,
I will love you until I die.

Chel-c Farmer (13)
Chalvedon School & Sixth Form College

Angels

Whatever happens through your days,
An angel is always there to stay,
They are there to sort your trouble out,
That's why they are always about.

When you are sad and feeling blue
Angels will be right there for you,
They wipe all of your tears away
And happiness will come your way.

Happy, sad, angry and blue
No matter what happens
They'll be there for you!

Rebecca Hewins (12)
Chalvedon School & Sixth Form College

Happy People

Little Lilly licks lollies like a little lady
Soppy Sam sleeps sweetly
Pretty Pearl picks pears
Awesome Andrea ate apples
Brilliant Becky bought bears

Happy people everywhere

Calm Cam caught Cameron
Happy Harry has hopes
Mad Maddie meets Margaret
Evil Emily eats eggs
Kicking Katie kept kuddles

Happy people are everywhere.

Chantelle Ralph (13)
Chalvedon School & Sixth Form College

My Favourite Person

As the wind blows I hear your voice,
And every time I see a bottle I think of you,
And I'll never forget the famous words,
Lord Admiral Nelson spoke,
'England expects that every man will do his duty'.
I think you have done this to the top
You taught me all about your younger life
Like HMS Rajah when you worked at the racing tracks and lots more.
As I look to Heaven, I see your smile
And know you are looking down on me
I will miss you and always love you!

My favourite person is my grandpa George!

Emily Snoding (12)
Chalvedon School & Sixth Form College

My Nightmare

I feel like I'm in a nightmare,
It is scarier than any of my dreams,
I'm not dead yet so that's a good thing!
That ghastly smell of decaying human flesh,
It smells like rotting eggs,
I hate it,
I feel so sick,
I can't get out,
I wanna get out,
Let me out.
I see the light,
Do I walk towards it?
Do I dare?
I walk towards it,
I see a house,
I run and I'm out.

Charlie Wallin (12)
Chalvedon School & Sixth Form College

Love

Love is like Heaven,
You are as lovely as a rose.
Your cheeks are as soft as a baby's bottom.
When you were young you were ugly
But now you're a swan.
I just want to say, I love you so much.

Kita Clark (13)
Chalvedon School & Sixth Form College

My Favourite Place

My favourite place is Jamaica,
One hundred miles of acres,
Birds whistling,
Snakes hissing.

When Bob Marley used to sing,
His fans always were listening,
In this wonderful kingdom
People were seeking words of wisdom.

Bob Marley got respect,
And never got the reject,
Bob Marley was a song writer,
He always had a lighter.

Bob Marley was always high,
He never ever wore a tie,
When Bob Marley began to sing,
He always had a bit of bling.

Sean Pittom (12)
Chalvedon School & Sixth Form College

Empty Ground

Dead flowers fly high,
So high they go into the sky,
Dead people on dark red ground,
Bang, bang, bang! Bullets fly by,
Hitting men and making some cry.

The sky was as red as Hell,
Most of the men fell,
Too many people gone,
Now there is no one,
Just blood and bone.

Aeroplanes flying,
People driving,
Men hiding.

Dogan Omer
Chalvedon School & Sixth Form College

Crunchy Crispie

Crispie is my pony,
Crispie is palomino,
Crispie is in a stable,
With two front shoes.

And that's Crispie.

Crispie can walk,
Crispie can trot,
Crispie can canter,
And throw me off.

And that's Crispie.

Crispie loves his dinner,
With apples and carrots,
He also loves his hay,
Soaked in water.

And that's Crispie.

Crispie is so friendly,
He's like a big dog,
He licks and kicks,
But gives me cuddles.

And that's Crispie.

Crispie can jump,
As high as a kangaroo,
But falls over his own four feet,
And loves to roll.

And that's *my* Crispie.

Sammy-Jo Brazil
Chalvedon School & Sixth Form College

Away With Words

I love my friends
I love to amend
Amend my friendships
And my friends

I love to shop
I love to shop till I drop

I love to chit-chat
However, I hate cats

I feel happy
I feel sad
Is this the best day I have ever had?

I want so many things
Clothes, diamond rings
And of course a bit of *bling bling!*

I want to live
I want to learn
Although I never want to burn

I want a husband
I want to be a wife
To lead a normal and happy life

To have children
To have a family
Now that would make life dandy

To live till I am old
To have such a goal.

Chloe Boyle (12)
Chalvedon School & Sixth Form College

The Pretty White Bird

Beautiful white wings,
Soaring through the sky,
'Look that's a dove,'
That's what I cry.

Gracefully swimming,
Through the cloudy blue pool,
'Look that's a dove,'
I shout as I'm trying to look cool.

The pretty white bird,
Passing me by
'Look that's a dove,'
That's what I cry.

Millie Levey (11)
Chalvedon School & Sixth Form College

Perfect Ponies

The stables, the stables, they run away with my words,
In Devon is where I go,
They gallop around fast, never slow,
We have to tiptoe around on our toes.

The smell can be foul,
But the sight takes it away,
For when you're riding the horse
There is no delay.

I get to ride Justy,
A great horse to ride,
She is the colour white,
And rides with perfect pride.

Then there is Solly,
She is white too,
Although she is smaller
She doesn't get you down in the blue.

That's about it for the stables right now,
But you should go there one day,
Don't worry about what's going to happen,
Because they will never get you down in the grey!

Abi Pullan (12)
Chalvedon School & Sixth Form College

Boys

A boy is a child forever.
A boy is a child who doesn't mind the weather.
A boy is a boy who doesn't care.
A boy is a boy who likes his chair.
A boy is a boy who wants to be cool.
A boy is a boy who likes relaxing by the pool.
A boy is a boy who likes some fun.
A boy is a boy who likes the sun.
A boy is a boy who likes his room.
A boy is a boy who hates using a broom.
A boy is a boy who loves to sleep.
A boy is a boy who likes exploring deep.
A boy is a boy who likes the mud.
A boy is a boy who likes making a thud.

So if you're a boy give your mum a break
You never know tomorrow, you may get a treat.

Cameron Greaves (12)
Chalvedon School & Sixth Form College

My School Poem

Sometimes you listen to a noise
before the object will appear in the playground
it is the same and these are some of the things I hear . . .

The stamping on the floor
the whistle of the wind
the opening of the gate
and the banging of the door
inside the classroom the sounds are softer
everyone can't wait to explode and blast off.
So you go and if you listen you will learn
but the one thing you must remember in school
is don't mess around and don't be a fool.

Jack Biggs (13)
Chalvedon School & Sixth Form College

West Ham United

Crowds chanting, cheering loud,
And in the sky was that horrible rain cloud.
When I came out of the tunnel the crowd went wild,
Every moment it was worthwhile.

West Ham scores, everyone gets off their seats
And all you can hear is the drum beats.
West Ham, always winning,
The crowd is always singing.

The crowd was singing . . .
1-0 down, 3-1 up,
That's how West Ham win the cup!

Luke Winter (12)
Chalvedon School & Sixth Form College

School

Let me go home my sweet lovely,
I hate that horrid school, that little old school,
Let me stay in lovely warm home,
Not out in the freezing cold,
My school looks like the grey, dull rain clouds,
At break time, at break time we stand around and do nothing
At break time, at break time it's so boring
It is home time, home time, now it's time to go home.

Zack Johnson (13)
Chalvedon School & Sixth Form College

School

B oard markers squeaking in my ear.
O ngoing speaking, I don't listen to it.
R eady to go home, but it is still 9 o'clock.
E ducation is a drag. I hate all lessons.
D ull and dreary, but it makes me weary.

Dale Basham (13)
Chalvedon School & Sixth Form College

The Sea

My favourite place is the sea,
I like to dive into the sea,
I like to swim in the sea,
I like to be in the sea,
I like the sea when it's rough,
I like the sea when it's calm,
I like the sea when it's clear blue,
I like the sea, I like the sea.

I like the sea when it looks like the sky,
I like the sea when it's cold and raining,
I like the sea when it's sunny and warm,
I like the sea when it's any weather.

I like the fish in the sea,
I like everything about the sea,
I like the dolphins and the whales,
The sea is where I want to be.

Samantha Rogers (12)
Chalvedon School & Sixth Form College

My Room

My bed is as warm as a desert,
My dog is as warm as a cover,
My carpet is as soft as a feather,
My room is as dark as the night sky,
My teddies are as big as a castle,
I feel as happy as a clown,
My love for my room is never down,
When I cry it's not for long,
It's because of a stupid love song.

Jessica Steward (12)
Chalvedon School & Sixth Form College

Friends

Friends, friends, friends,
They are funny, nice and caring,
They help you out when you are down,
They give you advice when you need them most.

Could you live without them?
As far apart as you and your friends will go,
The friendship remains in all of your hearts,
Friends, friends, friends.

Natalie Bohea (13)
Chalvedon School & Sixth Form College

The Beach

I love the sound of the waves crashing against the sea walls,
I love the smell of the ice cream stalls.

I love the way my dad smiles at me,
I love the way my brother runs straight to the sea.

I love the feel of the hot sand on my feet,
I love the way my mum packs the lunch neat.

I love the way my mum and dad sit down for a cup of tea,
I love the way the sun goes down into the sea.

I hate the way my mum picks up the phone,
Because I know that's when we have to go home!

Lorna Warren (14)
Chalvedon School & Sixth Form College

Shanice

Shanice is pretty and she is cool.
Shanice is repping for Chalvedon School.
She's with T-Van, she loves him so.
Sometimes she's a little slow.
This is my best friend I'm talking about.
She can be loud and even shout.

Jade Alden (13)
Chalvedon School & Sixth Form College

The Mystic Island

A mystic place out in the sea
The mystic island, can it be?
In the forest all the way down
Is a creature, all fat and purple and brown
Up the hill is the spelled goat
Who sings every word from his poor throat
By the bad old witch on the beach
Cooking spells, some of this and that, what about a leech?
In that cave there's a surprise
A dark shadow, a dragon inside
Unicorns run freely over the land
And the river, all smooth and grand.

James Busby (12)
Chalvedon School & Sixth Form College

Escape With Words

Cruel damnation
The meaning of creation
Smudged ink, white page
Trapped. Trapped. Inside a cage.
Only my feather and my ink
As dark and deep as a bottomless link
Called into a cold world
I must watch my life be unfurled
With no stop to this pain
I am sure I'll go insane
Just to escape
Wrap me in a black cape
My words dancing around me
With my quill and ink I see
Even though truly I am blind
My eyes are dead, they cannot find
But words I create today
My only way to get away . . .

Laranina Gillanders (12)
Chalvedon School & Sixth Form College

My One In A Million

Yes I know you think we're friends but I don't feel the same
Something happened yesterday, you are not to blame
I think I love you, somehow, some way, something changed
Yesterday this thought, this feeling like never before
You've won my heart and so much more
These are my confessions from my broken heart.

Annie Harvey (13)
Chalvedon School & Sixth Form College

My Dream World

Football's falling from the sky,
Goal post's landing upright.
Internet wires connect up high,
Computers everywhere in sight.
Playing on PS2 is like eating a pie,
On some games I have to fight.

In my dream world there is world peace,
Everyone loves sweets
And no one likes quiche,
No one gets beat.

Mitchell Stocker (12)
Chalvedon School & Sixth Form College

Babies Have A Way With Words

We babies have a way with words,
The older ones say our talk's absurd.
In every room there is a sun,
That's turned off and on by everyone.
Everything is big I see,
But not everyone's as small as me.
But anyway back to the talk,
That sounds like I've been eating chalk.
No one ever understands me,
But then again I'm just a baby.

They say my skin's as soft as silk,
Maybe it's because I drink this milk.
It tastes as if it's made of dough,
This makes this milk an awful foe.
But either way what the heck,
They still go shoving it down my neck.
Wait 'til I can really speak,
They'll say I have a lot of cheek.
But maybe they should enjoy these years,
Because the future's something they will fear.
Because when I can finally talk,
They'll be the ones that eat the chalk!

Alaina Smith (13)
Chalvedon School & Sixth Form College

Friends Don't Lie

The darkness enfolds me.
Every step of the way, fire sprouting beneath my feet
The soothing rain crashing against the floor creating puddles
I can't help but think of them
Think of what they have done to me
Non-believers

Over a picture
Over a stupid damn picture
No, it's not stupid
It's good.
But because of it
My friends don't lie.

They pick at me
Saying what they truly feel
It hurts inside; my heart is breaking into pieces I cannot pick up
I can't help this feeling
They don't regret what they have said
I just know it
I do . . .
I don't . . .

Alexandra Belcher (12)
Chalvedon School & Sixth Form College

Smile . . .

I love it when you smile,
Time we spend together will always be worthwhile.
Smile at me with your cheesy grin, it makes the hairs fall
From my chinny chin chin.
Please don't be sly,
It makes me cry,
If I do my dad said you will die.
It's only a joke,
And they were the words that I spoke.

Smile at me and make my day,
That's just an excuse for me to shout hooray!

Smile at me, my uncle owns a farm,
When I visited I caused a little harm.
The poor pig died,
But don't worry, it tasted good fried.

Smile at me as you're my friend,
Even though you drive me round the bend.

Smile at me I'm still a learner,
But when I'm older I will be a good earner.
Smile at me, you're really hot, even though I know I'm not.

Tanya Bolding (13)
Chalvedon School & Sixth Form College

Is It Because I'm Different?

Hi my name is Libby, but everybody calls me Lonely Libby
For I have no friends and the teachers can't see
That they beat me till I bleed
I go home at night, grab a knife for I believe it's what I need
People at the park call me Emo but I believe in a way
That they don't understand me, but they will one day
Then something possesses me to tell my mum and make her see
That this isn't a passing thing, it happens every day
And that makes me sad to say
My favourite place is a dark room and me on my own
Nothing but a knife and a phone
And if the phone rings I won't be able to answer at all
Because I have killed myself and I have fallen
To the fiery depths of Hell, for suicide is a sin,
Then I hear a bleeping noise and then I see a white ceiling
My mum smiles at me saying, 'You're back, we saved you,'
But no one knows how I'm feeling.

Chelsey Fox (13)
Chalvedon School & Sixth Form College

A Magical Chocolately Dream

Chocolate is like an edible fairy tale,
A magical chocolately dream,
Creamy, crunchy, crumbly chocolate,
A magical chocolately dream,
Melting inside a silvery wrapper,
A magical chocolately dream,
And then you see what chocolate
Really tastes like when it's inside your mouth
And you take a bite . . .
Then you realise it was a magical chocolately dream!

Rebecca Skerritt (12)
Chalvedon School & Sixth Form College

The Sweet Shop

I walk through the sweet shop door and head straight
                                      over to the side
That's where all the sweets are in different columns and lines
It is like being in Heaven, picking each sweet one by one
I just want to fall in these sweets, they make life so much fun
I wonder who invented them or how they were even made?
How did they make the colours and all the different shades?
When I'm older I'll have my own factory just like Willy Wonka's
Though it will be different, it won't turn me bonkers
I will have a chocolate fountain to drink from every day
'Just go for your dreams', that's what my mum would normally say
I walk out the sweet shop with all my bags of sweets
I can't save them for later, right now I have to eat
I look across the road and see the magazine and book shop
Did you hear about Billy Bopin? Once he started reading
                                        he simply couldn't stop!
I'm never going in there, I might catch that disease too
Nah, my opinion to magazines is a big fat boo!
It's time for me to go now unless you want me to get killed
My mum will be so worried, I'll need my brother as a shield.

Kayleigh Bradon (12)
Chalvedon School & Sixth Form College

Friends

Friends are the ones you love,
And are hard to get away from.
They help you with your ups and downs,
They always happen to be around.
All friends are as nice as pie,
All of them aren't even shy.
They are the ones you depend on,
Even though they can't sing a song.
All the girlies love to shop,
And blow their bubblegum till it pops.
So there is no need to lose your friends,
So make your friendship never end.

Jordan Cosburn (12)
Chalvedon School & Sixth Form College

There's A Monkey In A Tree

There's a monkey in a tree
Who tries to catch a bee

There's a cat on a mat
Who tries to catch a rat

There's a hog on a dog
Who tries to catch a frog

There's a snake on a rake
Who falls in the lake

There's a seed on a bird
Who tries to attack a nerd

There's a carp on a dish
Who's trying not to fart.

Josh Bailey (13)
Chalvedon School & Sixth Form College

The Soldier With Pie Eyes

The dusty road,
In the country lane,
A deadly battle,
Falls upon this plain,
No enemies in sight,
No need to fight,
Man I wish I had some pie!
A bullet flies, I flee to hide.
There is much to win in this battle,
Like fear to gain,
But the bullets of the enemy
Shall grant me no pain!

Later with cover of a Jeep,
I dream of a pie in the flavour of a sheep.
More bullets race by,
I fire back with a blind eye,
One soldier down,
To a friend I say goodbye
God I wish I had some pie!

A goldish brown
Of crispy light
I cannot win so I shall not fight.
I surrender for nigh is the night.
I get shot, I didn't even get my pie.

Jay Stone (13)
Chalvedon School & Sixth Form College

If Only . . .

If only I could turn back time,
I wouldn't have done my terrible crime.
The bullying had got too much,
All I said was, 'Can't you hush?'
The day I was home alone you came
And knocked on my door,
Then all of a sudden you punched me to the floor.
I was really mad,
All the time you made me sad.
So I went into the kitchen and grabbed the shiniest knife,
So that was the end of your life.
I'd finally won,
But in my life there wasn't any more sun.
You're blood-red as anger
If only I could turn back time,
I wouldn't have done my terrible crime.

Chloe West (12)
Chalvedon School & Sixth Form College

I Would Love . . .

I would love to be a monkey up there in the trees,
I would love to be a dolphin and sail the seven seas,
I would love to be a fox out there in the woods,
I would love to be a wolf and eat little Red Riding Hood,
I would love to be a sheep out there in the fields,
I would love to be a lion and never get killed,
But then again I would like to be a human,
I like the way I am!

Tara Pacey (12)
Chalvedon School & Sixth Form College

Sports

Sports are really good for you,
they get your pulse racing
and there are lots of other sports
like swimming,
even motor racing
that is a sport,
so there are lots of sports.

Josh Turner-Mason
Chalvedon School & Sixth Form College

The Big O

Smell the salt
Listen to the sound
Feel the cold mysterious water
Brush on your hand
This is the ocean
Might look so dreamy but the gloomy dark
That lies way down
Might not look so innocent
Sea creatures big or small
From sharks to krill
Some stay still
But don't be alarmed
This is all just the ocean
Big and blue
Fishermen love it
But do you?

Georgina Bailey
Chalvedon School & Sixth Form College

Baby Blue

Baby blue is the nice clear sky,
Baby blue is the deep blue sea,
Baby blue is a big huge bee,
Baby blue is new,
Baby blue is sweet like you.

Baby blue is a lovely day,
Baby blue is the sun shining all the way,
Baby blue are the eyes of a baby boy,
Baby blue is a word for joy.

Baby blue is all around,
Baby blue is upside down,
Baby blue is never a big huge frown,
Baby blue is to share,
Baby blue is a nice juicy pear.

Baby blue is the end of this poem,
Baby Blue is by Jacqueline Barnard.

Jacqueline Barnard
Chalvedon School & Sixth Form College

Storm

Clash, bang, rumble, slam!
The storm shows its rage,
The darkness overrides,
Animals cry and hide.

Darkness creepy and gloomy,
Like in a horror movie,
Children frightened,
Children scared.

Pitter-patter goes the rain,
On the roof, down the pipes,
Lightning breaks free,
Right over the sea.

Splish, splash, splosh,
Parents count their dosh,
Laughing with wonder,
Bang! goes the thunder.

The wind blows hard,
People on guard,
It's as cold as ice,
A few dead mice.

The storm starts to die,
Here comes the blue sky,
Children cheer,
Nothing to fear,
Summer's here.

Emily Gunn
Chalvedon School & Sixth Form College

I Will Always Belong

Walking along,
With a smack to my head.
It feels like I've
Got no cred.
But I carry on,
Try to be strong.
They keep on pushing,
But I know I belong.

This is the truth,
This is my story.
I do the work,
They get the glory.
Again they push on,
But I know I'm right
And I know they're wrong.
And then I tell them one thing,
I will always belong.

China Benton
Chalvedon School & Sixth Form College

Center Parcs

The happy feeling when I'm going on holiday to the best place.
I'm always thinking of what to do.
Only just arrived, hired bikes and here we are at the pool!
First the steep water slide, then the hot tubs,
Next the water shoots and rapid slides!
At three o'clock I'm dry, just getting used to my villa!
What we do all week is stay in the pool,
And when it gets dark we go to the bar above the pool,
And back to the villa, having an easy, silent night!

Elizabeth Cater (12)
Chalvedon School & Sixth Form College

Red

Red is the sound of poppies sprinkled around a summer's field.
Red is the feeling of your stomach after a nice glass of cherryade.
Red is the sound of blood dripping.
Red is the colour of a love heart pumping in your body.
Red is the taste of tomato puree poured in the Bolognese.
Red is the sunset burning in the horizon.
Red is the sound of tomatoes popping out the ground.
Red is the sign when you fail a test.
Red is the colour which flashes in your eyes when you cross a road.
Red is the sound of a devil laughing in the distance.
Red is the roar of a dragon waiting for food.
Red is the sound of fish jumping up and down in a misty lake.
Red is the feeling of walking down the seafront eating a saveloy.
Red is an emotion of a red ruby gleaming on your finger.

Alfie Smith (13)
Chalvedon School & Sixth Form College

Black

Black is a mystery waiting to unfold.
Black is a dark shadow filling you with fear.
Black is a creature that is misunderstood.
Black is a trap waiting to ensnare.
Black is a cat ready to pounce.
Black is a crow soaring up high.
Black is a night sky shrouding you in darkness.
Black is a reaper snatching your soul.
Black is a feeling you get when you're empty.
Black is a spirit that got lost on the way.

Black is a beautiful thing.

Shane Reynders (13)
Chalvedon School & Sixth Form College

Red

Red is hate, don't let it control you.
Red is to be misunderstood.
Red is love never-ending.
Red is love, wanting but can't have.
Red is passion burning inside you.
Red is inner anguish, in pain but no one to turn to.
Red is blood that keeps us living and breathing.
Red is a war just won, great victory comes with great sacrifice.
Red is being deceiving, don't trust it.
Red is a beautiful sunset after a bloody battle.
Red is a tall bright rose in a field of dull flowers.
Red is corruption killing off all happiness in your life.
Red is jealousy, wanting to take from a man
                        who worked hard for his wealth.

Luke Jones (13)
Chalvedon School & Sixth Form College

Black Is . . .

Black is friendship broken in two,
Black is as deep as a well,
Black is my mind gone blank,
Black is the sunshine hoisting through my veins,
Black is a broken heart,
Black is anger like a plain wall,
Black is the chills down my spine,
Black is the colour of my eye,
Black is the colour of love,
Black is the heavens up above,
Black is when my closest nan died,
Black is a gargoyle in the air,
Black is a giant teddy bear,
Black is a really bad migraine.

Luke Baker (13)
Chalvedon School & Sixth Form College

Diamond

Diamond
Precious, expensive
Gleaming, exciting-looking
Safe, cool, famous, cheerful
Shaping, sparkling, reflecting
Colourful, blinding
Crystal.

Dominic Niyazi (11)
Chalvedon School & Sixth Form College

New York

N ew York is a shopper's paradise, you just shop, shop, shop!
E verybody everywhere excited for what the day will bring.
W hat you do, where you go is up to you.

Y ellow cabs everywhere, driving around with so much care.
O ver there I see a celebrity filled with happiness,
   just had a baby called Cruz, oh! he's so cute.
R elax in a hotel for the night and eat a big kebab
   filled with joy and strength for the next day.
K atie Price, I saw looking at the Statue of Liberty.
   Oh, I wish I was there.

That's my dream, to visit New York.

Paige Goodgame (11)
Chalvedon School & Sixth Form College

Red

Out for a meal and you have red champagne
and after you have strawberry ice cream.
And the sun's out and people waiting to post their mail
and the place goes on fire.
And the fire engine comes and someone's bleeding
and blood comes out.
And putting on your lipstick, the cloud turns dark
and starts to rain and everybody's angry.
And putting roses in a vase,
these are all the things I think of when people say red.

Gillian Abbott (11)
Chalvedon School & Sixth Form College

Blue

Blue is the colour of the peaceful sky blowing away.
Blue is the sound of the ocean waves washing rapidly into the shore.
Blue is the pretty flowers swaying in the autumn winds.
Blue is the fresh plums blooming into season.
Blue is the big hungry shark that goes hunting for his food.
Blue is the dolphins jumping with pride.
Blue is the pretty pond coming to life.
Blue is the big colourful rainbow running away with colour.
Blue is the fresh damsons ready to pick, swaying on the tree.
Blue is the blueberry bush springing into life.

Charlotte Cater (11)
Chalvedon School & Sixth Form College

My Favourite Place

Candyfloss on a stick,
If you eat too much you will feel sick.

When I am high up on a ride,
It feels I am going to fall over the side.

The burgers at the theme park are really great,
When I see onions in them they make me want to faint.

The water ride makes me soaking wet,
That must be their best ride I bet.

When I go around looking for the best rides,
No, really, you cannot decide.

When I go on the dodgem cars to bump,
When they hit me I get a mighty thump.

When I have to go home,
I will go mental and moan.

When I get off the last ride,
I think I might run off and hide.

Dominic Villiers (12)
Chalvedon School & Sixth Form College

English

E nglish is a subject, one of my best, you may
N ot like it but you need it and it is fun if you have the teacher I have
G et to know her and you'll begin to like it yourself, if you don't
L ike it then you don't have this teacher, she
I s the best, she is Miss Murphy
S o do you like her? Everyone does, so
H ow is she? Is she good? Is she nice?

Kelly Plumpton (12)
Chalvedon School & Sixth Form College

War

War is bad
War is sad
When it's over we will be glad

Shooting guns and blazing fires
And cars as well with burst out tyres

I'll be glad when it's over
I won't miss the planes flying over

Blood and guts splashing everywhere
I close my eyes in despair

I'll be smiling when it's the end
Because it drives me round the bend.

Ryan Fredericks (12)
Chalvedon School & Sixth Form College

Battlefront

Guns fire like the speed of cheetahs,
the grass the men lay on is a wasteland,
we triumph over the enemy,
we triumph and defend our land,
the men cry as bullets fly,
we cheer as the enemy fall one by one
we remember those we love
and the love in our hearts make us keep on pushing.

Daniel Niall (12)
Chalvedon School & Sixth Form College

War

I am standing in a trench,
There ain't a bench in sight,
I can't wait till tonight.
I wish I was at home to use the phone,
Home sweet home.

Billy Cash (12)
Chalvedon School & Sixth Form College

Animals

There are all types of animals,
Big and small.
So many animals,
Some short and tall.

Lots of different animals,
Living in the sea.
So many animals,
Lots of little bumblebees.

Many different animals,
Underneath the ground.
So many animals,
Turning round and round.

Hannah Neale (13)
Chalvedon School & Sixth Form College

Cars

Muscle cars have a roar
Like a lion they thunder down the streets
As if they were carrying a storm.

Exotics look very nice
They can be just the same
But like lightning, quick as a flash.

Tuners can drift round corners
Gliding like hawks
Trying to catch their prey.

Jade Gutteridge (12)
Chalvedon School & Sixth Form College

A Love Poem

You are as pretty as a rose,
Our love is dazzling,
So it might be love, love and love.
Love is in the air for us,
Love is exciting
And love can make us be together.

Kelly Vince (13)
Chalvedon School & Sixth Form College

Olivia, Olivia

Olivia, Olivia you are as pretty as a rose,
Your long blonde hair is like the grass in the meadow
And your pure blue eyes are like the water in the seas.
I can't help thinking of my love for you.
The way you look is so dazzling.
I can't wait for our future together.

Jade Smith (13)
Chalvedon School & Sixth Form College

Love

L ove is sweet and kind.
O r love can be cruel.
V ery vicious love can hurt.
E veryone would like to be loved.

Jodie Padmore (12)
Chalvedon School & Sixth Form College

Dreams

While flying through the heavy sky
Trying to go high and high,
Looking down and seeing kites,
And seeing humans small as flies.
My dream's to fly.

Sailing through the heavy seas,
Heavy winds and the breeze,
Dolphins, seagulls I see all these,
No land to see or even trees.
My dream's to sail.

Travelling through the tall dark trees,
Cheetahs, tigers all to be seen,
They all run faster than the sea
All to get a little meat
My dream is to run with the wild.

So as crazy as our dreams can get,
Always remember not to forget,
That if our dreams may die,
You will always remember
About that time.

Annam Mehreen (12)
Chalvedon School & Sixth Form College

Away With Words

It makes me cry,
Seeing the innocent die,
To a disease they don't know,
An enemy, a foe.

It is depressing,
A whole world collapsing,
Swimming in a world of tears,
My mind drenched with fears.

Young kids,
In search of any figs,
To cure their disease,
Using the word please.

There are so many wars,
Behind closed doors,
There's no peace dove,
So where is the love?

There are so many twists and turns,
In the world,
I'm just a young girl,
Lost in a mind like a well.

Jennifer Frimpong (12)
Chalvedon School & Sixth Form College

My Dreamy World

Raindrops and candy canes,
Flowers and rainbows,
My world's the best,
No one's a pest,
I love my beautiful worlds.

People smiling at everything,
Everything and anything,
No one starving or crying,
No one hurting or dying,
I love my dreamy worlds.

Everything is perfect, yes perfect,
No one does wrong,
No arguing about money,
Or nothing so lonely,
I love my dreamy worlds.

But soon I sadly have to wake up,
And see this ordinary world,
No candyfloss clouds or candy cane trees,
Oh how I wish this world was real,
I love my dreamy worlds!

Charlotte Bettle (12)
Chalvedon School & Sixth Form College

What Should I Do?

How can I get past this?
Every day is the same.
The same questions. The same problems.
How can I solve this?
Time is passing me by . . .
Gears in my head, constantly, halting and jolting.

I open boxes . . . comparing . . . debating.
Is this really what I want?
Will it be OK on a day like today?
Will it hurt on a day like today?
Will it clash on a day like today?
I don't know what to do!

Old accusations run through my mind.
'Too many!' 'You're obsessed!'
I ask myself . . . is this true?
Just then, a smile breaks free across my face.
And I reply . . . 'No of course not.'

Not everyone understands why.
Not everyone feels the same.
Not everyone has tried to understand.
Not everyone will ever know.
And I don't care one bit.
It's my thing. Not theirs.

I now know what to do!
Finally. I've wasted enough time.
The questions that once ran through my head
Drift away with answers
The sparkling glitter shines on my face.
I'm going to wear my red Dorothy shoes.

Camie Broomfield (16)
King's Wood School

Untitled

Crisp under my feet
Everything has a chalk-like blanket
Untouched by human hands
Glistening in the light

The house doors open
Excited screams steal the silence
Footprints appear everywhere
The soft shimmering snow starts to fly

Angels on the ground being trodden on
Children running around frantically
Ducking, diving and rolling
Trying to escape the flying snow

It turns mushy
And sloshes under my feet
The white becomes grey
And the glistening fades

The excitement is short-lived
The blanket disappears
The untouched snow no longer exists
All that is left is waterlogged grass!

Toni Wicks (16)
King's Wood School

Leaking

A water bottle of memories,
Sprung a leak and dripping,
Forgetting things gone past,
Can't even remember tripping.

Well?
I don't remember . . .

My brain is like a sieve,
Broken,
Everything being filtered out,
Identity unspoken.

Well?
I don't remember . . .

When asked to recall the fondest
Or the oldest, nicest,
Images of nothingness are brought up instead,
Are they all blocked out due to dread?

Well?
I . . . don't remember . . .

Jack Cassie (16)
King's Wood School

Snow

I looked outside to see the weather,
I saw white stuff falling on the ground,
It was as quiet as a falling feather,
I believe it was snow I found.

April Bailey (13)
King's Wood School

The War

The war ends
and everyone goes out to see the bombed town,
they sit and sob
as the world comes to a standstill.
No one can move and no one can talk
all they do is sit and sob.

As time went on they became grateful
so glad and happy that they weren't killed
but sometimes
just sometimes
they would still sit and sob.

Caroline Murray (13)
King's Wood School

War

The streets are silent
The sky is dark
Everyone's hiding
Waiting to see if we die.

Noise in the distance
What could it be?
Hope they don't hit me
Sky full of lights now.

Air raid noise deafening
Ground shattering
Aeroplanes coming closer
Buildings crumbling.

Houses flattened
Homes gone
What is going on?
Oh my god! We are at war!

Lewis Thwaites (13)
King's Wood School

The Snow

The snow is white and glistening
All the children are playing,
With all their parents listening
We're so excited is what we are saying.

Everyone making snow angels
By laying in the snow,
The parents saying that's enough
The children saying no . . .

Everyone's enjoying their day,
In the snow it is so cold,
I'm sure everyone wants to play
Making snowmen you just can't hold.

It's time to finish and go in
Our clothes are soaking wet,
We have to throw our gloves in the bin
It will snow tomorrow I bet.

Kelsey Bridges (13)
King's Wood School

Society

The days have 'gorn'
when good manners was norm.

We don't have respect
with our dialect.

Many changes today
fill me with dismay.

Everyone has so much to say
but never in a polite way.

It's so unnecessary that we rebel
but there's no time to sit and dwell.

Some children are well behaved
but majority rave.

All we do is scream and shout
what we deserve is a good old clout!

Our manners are lacking
discipline is slacking.

If everyone was polite
we wouldn't have to fight.

It's not hard to believe
that we deceive

Us dudes are rude
and also rather crude.

Is this society today?
It shouldn't be this way.

If we work together we can bring manners back
and never let them lack.

Respect is gone
but it seems so wrong.

Lauren Stripling (14)
King's Wood School

The Bomb

As the sun started to set
planes filled the air.
They dropped their bombs
and slowly but surely
fell to the ground.
It was thunder to my ears.

Then there was a bang
followed by a cloud of smoke.
The cloud brought darkness to our lives
just like a cold, foggy winter's day.

Martin Cunningham (Davis) (13)
King's Wood School

Punishment

1 warning
1 punishment
1 whip on your hand
Tears on the eyes
Red marks on a stinging hand
The cane coming down
A stinger a girl got on the leg
Big red marks around the body
And that's one tough life.

Sam Harding (13)
King's Wood School

War

War is all around
When will the bombs start falling?
Nobody knows
People are all huddled in families and groups
Bang, crash, smash!
The bombs have started falling.

Francesca Morley (13)
King's Wood School

Lost

When you lose something close to you
It feels like it's gone forever
But sometimes it comes back
So people shouldn't say never.
Laughter and happiness, you
Keeping me sane in the head
Those three words you never speak
Are the words we need to keep.
But three words can't drown our fears
They can't wash away the river of tears

I feel like I've lost a part of me
Holding my teddy used to make me feel safe
My security blanket,
But now I'm older, stronger, wiser, braver
They say time heals all wounds
But that's not true
I got the pessimistic view.

They say what doesn't kill you makes you stronger
But time passes by and you're away for even longer
If you love something let it go
If it comes back it's yours for keeps,
That's what they say,
But when you're away
Inside of me I feel the loneliness beginning
Outside I watch the evening drawing in on me again
And we have to let it happen. We can say nothing.
When I'm with you colours seem to be brighter
I feel alive.
One thing we have to get is out of this life.

I've got my security back again
The other half of me.
Like the pepper to salt
Like Bill is to Ben
I'm going to hear those three words again.
Never say never,
Please say we'll always be together.

We're real,
Something only destiny has control of
Something that a single person can't prevent
But . . . shh! Mum's only gone for the moment!

Samantha Davies (16)
King's Wood School

Missing You

You were my best friend
I didn't understand
Why God took the good
And left the bad.

I cried for days
I just couldn't stop
You were the best
Always on top.

Why did you have to leave
And never return?
I can't survive without you,
But I have to learn.

For weeks and months
We just wanted you back
We still do now
And that's a fact.

It's been five years now
But the pain's still there
Everyone loves you
It just isn't fair.

You were the nicest
Person I knew
That was then
And it's still true.

We are so lucky
All of us are
Because you are the greatest
Grandad by far.

I know you're always there
Right behind us all
Ready to catch us
If we fall.

Harriett Ray (13)
King's Wood School

Bombs

Bombs, bombs everywhere
Banging, crashing at night,
I am sitting under the table
Shivering with fright.

Charlie Edwards (13)
King's Wood School

My Sister

What would I say if I was asked
What my earliest or worst memory was?
Well I know what I would say,
But what would you say?
I would tell you that the answer
To both of those questions is exactly the same.
It was when my sister was born.

My sister. A horrible treasure.
When she was younger
She was a cute bundle of joy,
But now she is an obnoxious rebellion.
She is the worst sister anyone could ever have!

Why would anyone want
A darling, devious devil for a sister?
Wouldn't you just want a darling younger sister?
This is what I have wished
For the last 10 years.

Every time I wish I had
A lovelier little sister,
I think about her when she was younger
And in fact,
I don't want to change her at all.

Katie Marsh (16)
King's Wood School

Misinterpretation

Like water in the rain
Whistling in the wind
Everything must stop at
One point in your life

From your first steps
To talking, to walking
Memories are precious in
A young child's life

I became weak
A target to the allies
No care to how my feelings were scorched
Burnt to ash
Reversing the pain is no question
Clocks move on
So should you!

Re-enactments would perform
In my subconscious
Clapping and cheering was blasted
But my skin stands still
No crack in my face, not one
Just glared at those who judge
Getting pleasure from other's misfortune,

Dents and colourings
Made my identity unknown to some,
Was I different
Or just misunderstood?

Years pass, gaining age,
Gaining confidence,
Gaining pride

To many personality is just a frame of mind
Not how one is perceived
The waistline shrunk
But the real me grew

It was always just me, me through and through.

Louise Reddington (16)
King's Wood School

Now An Adolescent

A toddler, at two I was teething,
At three I would sit by your side,
Have stories read to me at bedtime,
The gush of water running from my eyes.

A schoolgirl now, there is more to learn,
I have to leave your side,
The reflection of soldiering through the long days,
Memories shatter my heart for saying goodbye.

I am now an adolescent,
With the future gleaming at my feet,
If I choose to take the wrong path,
I will have to avoid defeat.

I am a long way off from knowing what life may have in store,
Rough edges softened by the dancing of the shore,
My knowledge is still growing, the glass is still cloudy,
Still I am now sure,
But there is plenty of room for more.

Now I am an adolescent I will reflect upon my life,
And have a greater understanding of how to do things right.

The shadow still lays behind me,
Like the footsteps of a stalker,
The pain is a stabbing knife,
But I am older now . . . yes older,
I will have to leave this behind.

From misty winds to sunny spells,
I crave of a clearer view,
Of what I will be in the future,
Will the shiny spells come true?

It is me standing at the top of the mountain,
Yelling, 'I have made a success!'
From shiny, sharp reflections,
I will do my best.

As I stare in this mirror and review my thoughts,
The sudden gush of the waves hit me,
And clears up all of my thoughts.
It tells me,

An image of what I will become,
Of all what I want to be,
Of all the things I have wished for,
I am glad of what I am, I am me.

Lucy Cadby (15)
King's Wood School

Orbiting

I am but one person
Even though sometimes I feel like two
Like I'm split - split right down the middle
The two people in me are the same
Yet so different - they are their own person.

They make me, without them I'm nothing.
And nothing is full.

Many things make a person,
Like lots of things make a galaxy or the universe
Like family, friends and happiness
With me,
It's all three
And much, much more.

They make me, without them I'm nothing.
And nothing is full.

I need friends like the night needs a moon.
My friends are my whole world, my galaxy, my universe
My night and day
When I'm sad they're there for me
And happiness

follows me. Like a ray of light.
Reflecting
Absorbing everything happy and everything bright
Banishing all darkness and sadness
They are my stars in my sky.
My sun in my day.
My happiness. My all

The two people in me are now complete,
whole, sealed
and secure.
They are the air that I breathe.

They make me, without them I'm nothing.
But my nothing is non-existent.
I am full.

Georgina Pope (15)
King's Wood School

A Shout Out To Mother

From the moment I saw the Earth
I knew I was going to learn
Not knowing how to grow up
Or which way to turn.

Passionate, pure, Precious you named me.
Living the life of love - all this
You shared with me!
I'm a fruit that popped from your tree.
You watered it, fed it,
But never spoilt it.

The Devil tries to hold me down
But you show me the way.
I told you I was troubled
And you told me to hold my troubles
And throw them away.
When sorrow took its toll
You said to me, never look away
Quite a strange thing to face
But you taught me a better phrase
 . . . See you when you get there . . .
 . . . I mean the better place!

Mother Nature, blossomed
From thee mother tongue
My identity is your creation
From the beginning to the end.

Precious Sibanda (15)
King's Wood School

Troubles

I have very few troubles,
And I almost never overreact,
But if I do ever have any annoyances,
You had better watch out!

One thing I hate is sandals and socks,
I wish they were gone,
I want them under key and lock!

Another thing I hate are brothers and sisters,
They annoy me so much,
If they were shoes, they would give me blisters!

Something else I hate is posh, perfect people,
I want them to burp,
Or slip up in public!

The thing that I hate most is . . .
Brothers and sisters, acting posh,
Wearing sandals and socks,
Drinking my favourite drink, in the middle of winter, with company over!

I have very few troubles
As you can see . . .
I almost never overreact,
But if you do get on the wrong side of me
Simply leave me be!

Morgan Power (11)
St Bernard's High School, Westcliff-on-Sea

The Poem Of The Bakerloo Flea

This is the poem of the Bakerloo flea,
The Bakerloo flea that grew six foot three,
The Bakerloo flea was ginormous,
The flea was bigger than a rhinoceros.

The Bakerloo flea stunk,
More or less of a skunk,
The Bakerloo flea was scary,
But atrociously hairy,

The Bakerloo flea lived underground,
That's until Bob came round,
He came with some spray,
Everybody would pray
That this would be the end of the Bakerloo flea,
Bob sprayed,
Residents prayed,
Yes! That was the end of the Bakerloo flea.

Residents threw a parade,
Everyone shouted hip hip hooray,
Everyone was happy,
Even the baby in a nappy.

Sophie Wizik (12)
St Bernard's High School, Westcliff-on-Sea

Going To A Restaurant

For starters, I really couldn't choose
Whether to have the salmon or soup.
Spaghetti Bolognese
Or egg mayonnaise.
Pasta diavolo,
Mushrooms and prawns,
Or even lasagne.

Main course came after,
Now here's a disaster.
There's steak and there's chicken,
There's veal and there's fish,
And millions of vegetables,
All in a long list.

Then there's the drinks
Oh what will I pick?
Apple juice, Coke, water or a tonic,
Or maybe a wine,
That sounds divine.
There's Della Casa,
Frascati or rosé.
There's Lambrusco Rosso,
Chianti or Corvo.
But I don't want to see the bill when I pay,
So I think I'll just stick with a nice lemonade.

For dessert it was simple
A chocolate fudge gateau,
And then just to go, a decaf latte
But I couldn't pay, so now I work there all day.

Vittoria Murphy (11)
St Bernard's High School, Westcliff-on-Sea

Tonight Was Different

As I walked through the door,
He was there ready and waiting.
His knife in his hand
And murder in his eyes,
Tonight felt different.

I have scratches up my arms
And bruises on my legs
With a big black eye.
From knives
And punches

Shoved and pushed
I hit the wall
Then with his knife
He scratches me
And twists my ankle

My mum steps through the door,
Laughing she opens a bottle of lager
Gives one to him
And then he gets angry
Then hits with his whip

My mum shouts, 'Dinner!'
Then he goes
Locks the door
No dinner for me tonight

Standing there on my own
Nowhere to go
I see the knife
And then blood comes out
I am dead!

Jasmine Davison-Holmes (11)
St Bernard's High School, Westcliff-on-Sea

If I Could Turn Back Time

If I could turn back time
Into the day,
When I was a young girl
And all I did was play!

'Fun' was the word
That most people liked,
Everyone said it
It made them all psyched!

Things have changed
From the past,
There is a bit of fun
It'll never last!

In those days
There were no wars,
No one got angry
They didn't show their claws!

I wish that I could turn back time
Into the day,
When I was a young girl
And all I'd do is play!

Shannon Wood (12)
St Bernard's High School, Westcliff-on-Sea

A Sad Tale, A Happy Ending

Trudging along the cold winter streets
Following people in hopes of a treat
The snow was freezing my tiny paws
And sludge was sticking to my unshapely claws.

My fur was all ruffled and layered in ice
I saw people and pavements, and rubbish and mice.
Shivering and bedraggled I wandered around
My stomach was rumbling, I yearned to be found.

I slunk to a deep dark corner, my whiskers a mess
My heartless old owners just couldn't care less.
I bet they were all warm and cosy at home
But what about me, frightened, cold and alone.

I had just got comfortable on a makeshift bed
Curled in a ball, thinking of what I'd like to be doing instead
I imagined and imagined until it felt weird
The snow started falling, my thoughts disappeared.

A fog surrounded sun rose higher in the sky
Sleepy eyes saw a girl close by
Then a freckled, friendly face smiled as it appeared
Now I knew there was nothing to be feared.

Chloe Guest (13)
St Bernard's High School, Westcliff-on-Sea

It's My Life

The premiere awaits me,
With everyone at sight,
The photographers call me,
As I enter a wonderful night.

When I get out they're there again,
Flashing their cameras about,
Trying to get an embarrassing picture
Of one of us.

Don't they have somewhere to go,
Somewhere to be instead of following me around all day?
They're outside my house,
Outside my parties, everywhere we go they are.

Walking into a local shop,
That is where I can see,
On the front of the papers,
Is a picture of me.

Some people like this,
But I certainly don't,
I need my own life,
Not only my job.

I've had enough of this right now,
I've got to get away,
I need to start a new life,
Where no one knows my name.

Chloë Wells (12)
St Bernard's High School, Westcliff-on-Sea

The Forgotten Friend

So here I sit,
On a shelf full of books,
Losing all of my beautiful looks.
My pages are crinkling,
My cover is wrinkling,
I become more forgotten every day.

I used to be your friend so dear,
You used to hold me very near.
How long do I have to wait,
For that special date,
When you will confide in me?

There were many times in the day,
When you walked the other way.
I did not flee,
When you came and turned my key,
I let you stay and confide in me.

Oh I cry, oh I whimper, so sad am I,
But no matter how I complain,
Nothing will ever be the same,
So here I sit on a shelf full of books,
Losing all my beautiful looks.

Claudia Devlin (13)
St Bernard's High School, Westcliff-on-Sea

In The World

In the world around me,
I see violence, destruction and war.
All the people that surround me,
Are asking for more, more, more.

More money for clothes,
For a fabulous look,
More money for reading,
A wonderful book.

Yet also the world is beautiful,
Full of vibrant colour and life.
I want to explore this world further
And rid the world of hunger and strife.

Mary Imbush (12)
St Bernard's High School, Westcliff-on-Sea

Through The Eyes Of . . .

Alone in a world,
so humble a place,
besides my frail brother,
so gaunt in his face.

Inheriting the disease,
of one which rules over,
infects an innocent life,
he turns to my shoulder.

Seeing the suffering
through the eyes of my brother,
his heart full of love,
to offer to no mother.

His fragile body,
lying weak on the floor.
A lifeless figure,
who can be helped no more.

Desperate for food,
as we struggle to survive,
fighting an endless battle,
which has dictated our whole lives.

Left alone in a world,
so humble a place,
holding my dying brother,
I wipe a tear from his face.

Melanie Horton (14)
St Bernard's High School, Westcliff-on-Sea

The Lonely Moon

Cold and lonely, way up high,
not to be seen in the daylight sky,
dangling alone, but I do not fall,
but I'm an outcast here because my friends are so small.

From way up here I see all that goes on,
from walking a dog to a man screaming, 'John!'
From a lady in an argument shouting on the phone,
to a little girl crying, lost from her home.

But each night when everyone's having tea,
a man comes to the beach to look up at me,
having a friend how proud I feel,
but I'm just a rock and he is real.

Emma Nee
St Bernard's High School, Westcliff-on-Sea

Hard Questions, Worse Answers!

Is Mum crying?
Have we still got a TV?
Are the bills in the dishwasher?
Did the council hear our plea?

Is Dad with Tracey?
His female friend,
Is it true?
Has Mum gone round the bend?

Did Dad kill a man?
Is this social worker for real?
Dad did say that prison,
Gives a bed and three meals.

It's too much to bear,
Mum put a knife to her wrist.
Heaven will be lovely
But oh, she will be missed!

So Dad's in prison,
Mum, well she's dead.
I'm not on the streets,
But in care instead!

Sarah Arnold
St Bernard's High School, Westcliff-on-Sea

The Seven Ages Of Man - Modern Version
(Based on a poem from William Shakespeare's 'As You Like It')

Not known to the world, he is so small
Not understanding life, not at all
The book of life is just beginning
Young spirit, joy and hope bringing
If he knew what life would bring
Then a different song that he may sing
Young baby of God's creation
Another being waiting with anticipation

As he grows his days go on
He starts to learn, to talk and to walk
His life is far ahead, still long
It is the start of a beautiful song
Such an interested mind
No time to be bitter and unkind
Like a flower just blossomed on a beautiful summer's evening
His parents are so happy, they give joy, dance and sing

The next stage of this boy is another chapter of his book
He spends muddy days in the park
Playing kick about and climbing on the bark
Enjoys sunny days with his mum and dad
Everyone says what a lovely lad
He is like a tornado, so full of life
He makes new friends in school, takes life in his stride
He is ambitious and does well in his studies
Mum and Dad are happy with him and his choice of buddies

Onto the new part of the story he can tell
He mixes in with the wrong crowd
Thinks he is so cool but really he is just rude and loud
Wants to scream aloud and to rebel
And he is like a volcano waiting to go bang

Mum moans about his attitude and the way his clothes hang
He starts to steal, swear, lie and wear a hood
Deep down he can tell he is doing so much bad and no good
His life at the moment is a black hole
And he is falling down and down
He doesn't smile anymore,
It is like on his sad face there is a painted scary frown

But eventually he becomes an adult and is much more mature
He is like a record that has been switched
He parties hard, having fun, his pitiful life has been ditched
Moves out of his home and gets a car
A promotion here and there, taking him afar
Meets a woman who becomes his wife
Having good times and enjoying his wonderful life
His life is a leaf that has been turned over,
He makes everyone proud
Now he has no need to feel spite and be nasty, cruel and loud

Now he gains some more years to add to his lifetime
His life is a ticking clock and all the times the good
And bad moments of his journey to get him there
He has three children who laugh and cry and play and cheer
His life is so complicated and busy,
Not quite making sense like an abstract painting
He loves his family and home and has everything
That he has been waiting for, his children grow and move away
He grows older and wiser each and every day
He and his wife move to the beach and have some grandchildren,
The golden years are here now to stay
He really loves the book he has created himself this way

His life is like a giant jigsaw puzzle and this is the last piece
The world is such a scary place
He has been through happiness, sadness, joy, peace and disgrace
He walks along the sandy shores
The lapping waves are his memories
Washing in and then away again
Where he watches them disappear forever
His wife is gone, he feels so alone
The scary teenagers all carry a knife and wear a hood
Their hearts are still and motionless with no compassion, like wood
He looks into one of their faces
And sees a mirror of himself in his youth
At last he finally learns the sad and disgusting truth
Of what life can be really like
The jab with what felt like a sharp pike
Hit him in the head, they don't even care, because he is dead.

Sophie Bell (12)
Sawyers Hall College

Emotions

My sadness is like an endless black hole,
It goes on forever,
My love is like a gleaming sapphire,
It never stops shining with light,
My happiness is like a person with a contaminated disease,
It's locked up inside,
My jealousy is like a huge ball of green gas,
It fills my head and makes me explode,
My anger is like Hell,
A rage of a thermal abyss.

Lucy Webber
Sawyers Hall College

My Private Cloud

Me,
Just sitting there,
On my little cloud,
Floating away,
From all my fears,
'Cause it's just me,
On my private cloud.

Holly Nott (12)
Sawyers Hall College

Jack Is Back!

Jack Sawyer, what a pest!
He's my brother, and not the best!
All he does is moan, moan, moan!
Horrid remarks, groan, groan, groan!

He always has to get on my nerves,
Although, when he's told off,
He gets what he deserves!

Ha ha! I laugh at him,
His hilarious jokes,
About some teacher, Jim!

He isn't all bad,
Sometimes he's great!
But, I usually think,
Is it unreal or fate?

People say that we are alike,
But I say, 'No, no!'
Go on, on your bike!

His favourite saying is,
'Run along silly'
But I ignore him,
Because I like my dress frilly!

A rebel without a cause,
Is what Dad calls him,
Even 'criminal' he shortens down to 'crim'!

What a legend!
I do have to say,
As he was born,
The month after May!

Jack is here now,
No doubt about that!
So I won't say anything,
Just silent, silent as a bat!

Lily Sawyer (13)
Sawyers Hall College

The World In The 21st Century

He snorts and sniffs lots of glue,
If you're rich he will mug you,
He wears his hood in the street,
Looking down at his feet.

He is a massive thug,
Getting high on drink and drug,
Playing his music nice and loud,
Pick-pocketing from bustling crowds.

Watch your back, he has a knife,
He is prepared to take your life,
Killing is so easy,
He will never get queasy.

That is what the world is now like.

Jack Foulger (13)
Sawyers Hall College

The Game

Walking through the tunnel
In a big bundle,
The atmosphere is ecstatic
In a big panic.

Preparing for kick-off
Hearing that awkward cough,
The pitch is like a perfect cut emerald
An emerald cut to perfection.

The tension builds up
Killed by crucial mistakes,
Like a rabbit attempting to pass through a pack of foxes
A crucial mistake costs the rabbit its life.

As the tension of the game builds up
The crowd will become more alive,
The volume of the stadium will change
The atmosphere of the game is changing.

The outcome of the game could be decided by the crowd
The crowd motivates the players and makes them proud
The crowd is like the teams' fuel, keeps them going
Like petrol in a car keeps it going till it's finished.

Bambo Banjo (12)
Sawyers Hall College

My Seven Ages
(Inspired by a poem from William Shakespeare's 'As You Like It')

All the world is a massive lake
All the fish just swimming about
They all come and go
Eating everything in their path
They get hooked and then let go
Never to be seen again

At first the toddler drowning, Daddy pulling him out
Then the crying schoolboy begging not to go
The school is just up ahead, its wide doors open
Waiting to eat them all

And then the girlfriend waiting in the bus stop
She cannot see you so she leaves you forever

And then the teen is becoming mature
Will he ever meet the right girl?
Across the road, are his eyes deceiving him?
The girl of his dreams
He runs to her and kisses her
She faints

Then he takes her hand and walks with her round the lake
He falls in once again, struggling to get out
He gets caught up in the weed and goes under
He cannot get up
He goes deeper and deeper
Until he sees no more and drifts off forever.

Jake Kimberley (12)
Sawyers Hall College

I See, I Hear, I Smell

I see a large playground.
I see lots and lots of children crowded around someone.
I see a man giving out sweets
And letting children enter the dinner hall first.
I see man in a red apron and tanned skin.
I hear children playing football and girls giggling.
I smell food, lovely food, burgers and chips.
I also smell the strong smell of vinegar
Trickling on the burgers and chips. Mmmm.
I see . . . I see . . . wait, I see . . . my *dad*.

Michael Watts (12)
Sawyers Hall College

The Path

I see two paths,
Both are completely different,
I must choose which one to take,
After I take it I know there's no going back.

One path is dead and been used,
The black crows are waiting there,
There's no telling what's lingering in the darkness,
All I know is that it's been used before.

The other path is full of life,
The grass green and healthy,
I can see everything there
And I know that no one had used it before.

Now I have to make a decision,
Do I take the path that has been used
Or do I take the path that hasn't,
I want to try something new,
But there's no telling what's there.

When I take a path I know,
There's no going back,
So I must think about it carefully,
Or my life will not be worth living.

Jamie Kingston (12)
Sawyers Hall College

The Works

The works of a man, the ocean and sea.
The works of a caterpillar, you and me.
All works are the same, elbow, leg and knee.
The works of a man, the ocean and sea.

The works of the moon, stars and the Earth.
The works of a baby's cry at their birth.
All works are the same, even a Smurf.
The works of the moon, the stars and the Earth.

The world's population all have works.
The world's population, most are jerks.
The works of a man, the ocean and sea.
The works of a caterpillar, you and me.

Joe Ward (12)
Sawyers Hall College

Ride Of My Life

I jumped on his back,
Off he went.
He galloped on fields,
Then jumped over the fence.

We slowed to a walk,
When we came to a beach.
Down the rocky mountain,
And way out of reach.

He goes again,
Straight through the sea.
Water splashed,
All over me!

At last it was time,
To go back.
That was the end,
Of my wonderful hack!

Charlie Parker (13)
Sawyers Hall College

The Man From Timbuktu

The man from Timbuktu,
He only had one shoe,
He hopped all night,
He hopped all day,
The man from Timbuktu.

The man from Timbuktu,
With one old, tatty shoe,
Tripped over a rock,
Lost his shoe and his sock,
The man from Timbuktu.

The man from Timbuktu,
With no socks and no shoe,
Sat cold and afraid,
Alone in the shade,
The man from Timbuktu.

Gabby Wallace (12)
Sawyers Hall College

Hawk Eye

High in the sky,
I look for my prey,
With children to feed,
I don't have a choice,
Soaring through the clouds,
Free as the wind,
I spot something,
I swoop down for a closer look,
Vultures scarper,
There's not much left,
Taking off again,
I feel freedom,
I go wherever I want to go,
I do whatever I want to do,
Darkness covers the sky quickly,
I head back home,
My children will live the same as me,
But will go hungry tonight.

Fern Royffe (13)
Sawyers Hall College

War

Here I am back in war
Hearing guns and engines roar

Bangs and explosions as I hit the deck
I have a look, still all in check

Death all around
Many still to be found

Chattering as I fire my gun
Even though the deed was done

As I return home
My platoon having a moan

At home we are greeted by a roar
Even though we could have done more.

Sam Sparks (13)
Sawyers Hall College

Rainy Days

Rainy days
 Rainy days,

  Thunder loud
   Lightning quiet,

    Wet roads
     Dry homes,

      Rainy days
       Rainy days,

        Toasty fires
         Freezing winds,

          Slanting trees
           Moving leaves,

            Rainy days
             Rainy days.

Kieran O'Shea (12)
Sawyers Hall College

Sport

The basketball is a giant orange
Bouncing around the table
And jumping into the bowl
Bananas grab at it
But many don't succeed

The tennis ball is a small moon
Shining around the stadium
Stars whack it
And hope it will catch their opponent off guard
Whack, whack, whack

The football is a pen lid
Being hit by the pens
They try to get it into the bin
But the pens run out
And then the lesson ends

A race car is a leaf
Caught in a tornado
Round and round it goes
Picking up speed at every turn
Catching up with the other leaves.

Ryan Bishop-Olejnik
Sawyers Hall College

Bike Ride

We're going on a bike ride,
We're going to see the sea.
Seagulls flying past,
The boats are very fast.
We'll ride along the pier,
But we'll have no fear.
We're going on a bike ride.

Keeleigh Hogan (13)
Sawyers Hall College

Chocolate

One square or two
it's up to you

because when you are sad
it will always make you go mad.

Three square or four
or even eat more.

You could have it in a cake
or even in a shake.

Lily Bolden (12)
Sawyers Hall College

Untitled

Skiing down a mountain
lost for words
skiing down a mountain
can't be disturbed
skiing down a mountain
can't see any grass
skiing down a mountain
I'll never give it a pass.

Elle Jopson (12)
Sawyers Hall College

A Lonely Child

I am a lonely child sitting in a separate corner of the class,
I am struggling with my work,
Nobody pays any attention to me, not even my teacher.

At break I am lonely and go and sit by myself,
All around I can hear cheers of happy laughter,
And I can see boys playing football and girls chatting.

I wonder to myself, am I invisible,
Can anyone else actually see me,
People ignore me and I don't know why, what have I done wrong?

I might be quiet and I might be shy
But I still have my own thoughts and feelings,
So just let me join in, I want to have fun.

I see a group of boys heading my way
I begin to feel scared
But the boys stand in front of me and say,
'Come and sit with us, don't be on your own.'
This really made my day and I'm not lonely anymore.

Amy Richards (13)
The Gateway Academy

Mechanics

As a mechanic I fiddle with nuts and bolts,
I tinker with old car parts,
I search for any sign of faults.

As a mechanic I check the oil flow,
I change the oil filter,
I check if anything's wrong below.

As a mechanic I replace car doors,
I replace car windscreens,
I make sure the car's not too close to the floor.

As a mechanic I check that the engine is working,
I check that the pistons are all moving,
I try to make sure that the car doesn't keep choking.

As a car I keep breaking down,
I keep running out of petrol,
Both of these things make me frown.

As a car I need fixing a lot,
I like my mechanic,
He always hits the spot.

As a car I have fun driving up and down the ramps,
It hurts a little when my mechanic checks my exhaust fumes,
But not as much as being in a crash and ending up as scraps.

As a car I'm tired at the end of the day,
I've had all my fun,
And as some say, it's time to hit the hay.

Craig Madle (13)
The Gateway Academy

Through The Eyes Of The Tiger

As I creep along my familiar route through the jungle,
I hear a strange noise . . .
Was it a bird?
Or could it be an animal on foot?
Or a monkey swinging in the trees?
The noise was definitely getting louder
And sure enough, it was my worst enemy - poachers!

I saw them glance in my direction
And as I stared back
I could feel the hairs on my back stand on end
The hot sun was beaming down on me.

Suddenly, dozens of spears started flying in my direction
I ducked beneath the closest bush,
And then slowly crept through the foliage
Trying to camouflage myself as best I could.

I quickly dashed across the open plain,
More spears were flying in my direction,
I dodged them and then staggered into a ditch

I could still hear the poachers running
I got away this time . . .
Next time I might not be as lucky . . .

Hayley Bannister (13)
The Gateway Academy

Coloured

What is the meaning of coloured?
I know what colours are.
But what is coloured?
Does it mean when something is coloured in?
I don't think so.

Why did she call me that?
Why did she yell it at me in front of all them people?
Does it mean something nasty?
Does it mean something nice?
How am I supposed to know?

Why did she say it?
She doesn't even know who I am.
Why did she laugh afterwards?
It must be something bad
I just know it.

Why would she say that though?
'Coloured' I've heard that word somewhere
But I just can't remember
Let me refresh my mind.

Oh, that's it
I remember now
My friend was called 'coloured'
She told me what it meant
But, but . . .
She couldn't
How could she
I understand now!
I'm a nought
She's a cross.

Jessica Ingando (13)
The Sydney Russell School

9FS Is Different Than The Rest

Exciting! Walking in K22,
And start to think about the funny jokes:
'Hello class and Dami,' Tutor says.
Some people laugh and some just sit and stay.
I keep smiling, wondering, what is next?
Ryan screaming loudly, 'I am gorgeous'
Huh, I bet he thinks that is funny, not.

After first bell I go and find my friends:
Elle, Lauren, Kirsty and Megan have . . .
Hair coloured by the sun's yellow warmth.
Sir, is no competition to Cealey.
When it comes to fashion and looking good.
Dami says 'Your mum' very often now.
Mwenya giggles like a little birdie,
Chengetie and Jessica can't shut up
Cos they've got big mouths, blah, blah, blah.
Now you know about the girls.

But it is time to talk about the boys
Ricky Smith is the ginger haired one.
We could never lose him on trips
Cos we can spot him from a mile far away.
Andrew and Lewis are the tiny ones,
But their mouths don't stop yapping in class.
Ashley's always quiet while in lessons,
But outside everyone can hear him shout.
Ben was on report once or twice last year
But now he has learned his lesson well enough.

If you ever read this poem 9FS,
Just remember you're the best.

Vesela Maslenishka (14)
The Sydney Russell School

Colour-Blind

What am I?
Blank.
Coloured.
I am not a rainbow.
I am not a sheet.
So who the hell are you to tell me what I am?
It's who I am.
It's what I like.
It's . . .
It's not my skin.
I am not my skin.

Go away. Leave me.
Run from my skin.
I don't care.
Think I'm strange.
Strange to who?
I don't care.
Blank or coloured?
Figures, fools,
Work it out.

Coloured says 'blank'.
Blank says 'coloured'.
You damn fools!
Don't hate what you see.
Hate what's inside.
Hate my guts.
I am not blank.
I'm not just coloured.
So what am I?

Esther Osarfo-Mensah (14)
The Sydney Russell School

Pain

Bruises, cuts and bumps,
Kicked like a ball.
Beaten to the bone,
'Please stop!' I call.

My heart is aching,
From all those names.
'Ugly! Stupid! Retard!'
They all say I will burn in flames.

Me and my husband both love her,
But why does she always yell?
We ask her what is wrong,
She just mutters, 'I'll never tell . . .'

Me and my wife must discipline her,
To make her understand!
But she never ever listens,
I'm forced to give her hard kisses on her hand!

There was blood on my bed,
When my father was done.
Touching and hurting me,
The respect for him . . . I have none!

Sitting on the roller coaster of pain,
There is no escaping this terrible ride!
Will my pain ever end
Or will I always have to hide . . .?

Manpreet Kaur Hunjan (12)
The Sydney Russell School

Giving

Why?
Calling me, every day
Asking
Need something
Never offered
Why?
If not,
Selfish!
Why?
Feel like am in an empty room shouting
But not being heard!
All these feelings left behind
Can't take it anymore
I can cut things in two
Like Mary Shelly's Frankenstein monster
Oh why!
Can't take it anymore
I should have stopped it when it started
That's selfish
Oh why!
I feel entangled in a spiderweb
Lost in a maze
Why?
I just want to be free
Of all of these things
I want to be able to move
I want to be able to have time for me
Lastly, I want to be me,
Without being selfish in any way
I want to give, without being pulled or held back!

Akyaa Boakye-Ansah (13)
The Sydney Russell School

Maniacal Egocentric Nincompoops!

Piles of dirty dishes in the sink,
always asking, 'Honey, another drink?'
Maniacal Egocentric Nincompoops!
Going to work every day,
'You can't do a man's job, kitchen's that way.'
Maniacal Egocentric Nincompoops!

When asked to mow the lawn,
they say, 'What?' with a yawn.
Maniacal Egocentric Nincompoops!
Dinner time, barbarically eating with his mouth open,
burping and farting, the silence broken.
Maniacal Egocentric Nincompoops!

Dirty underwear and clothes all on the floor,
stinking out the bedroom more and more.
Maniacal Egocentric Nincompoops!
Bank accounts and spare cash, only he keeps,
always spent on beers for him and his creeps.
Maniacal Egocentric Nincompoops!

Restricted to go out,
never stops having doubts.
Maniacal Egocentric Nincompoops!
He says, 'Every day I work really hard.'
'You have to respect me; it's not easy being a guard!'
Maniacal Egocentric Nincompoops!

He's always right; it's always his way,
'You cannot visit your mother without my say!'
Maniacal Egocentric Nincompoops!
Flowers in hand, chocolates in a shiny tin,
rushing to put on the TV, 'Arsenal might win.'
Maniacal Egocentric Nincompoops!

Gurleen Kaur Hunjan (14)
The Sydney Russell School

My Father

My father strolls to the gymnasium
To work out and to exercise
Expertise in a human form
He likes to train his body and mind

Building up his abdomen and arms
Every day getting stronger
Bigger and bigger, getting more powerful,
He is getting fitter and livelier.

Life has never been so good
His life is getting better
He has a lot of confidence
And he has never seemed so happy.

My father recently turned 40
But he is still as strong
And more lively than ever
And it is true what they say

Life really does begin at 40
My dad is really happy now.
Life is brilliant and I wouldn't have it,
Any other way!

Kyle Powell (15)
Woodbridge High School

I Do Still Love You

The way she was so unique,
Just the intelligent, but cool way she would speak
I truly loved her.

We would stay up late
I thought I was annoying her,
But she would never complain
We often got the giggles
Which would drive my mum insane!

Her dancing is what I admired the most
Yeah, my sister dances for Ne-Yo,
Oh the way I used to boast.
Always encouraging me to keep on with my dancing,
She had faith in me.

She would take me to her classes
Teach me all her latest dances
And her friends would enjoy my company,
I thought I was ten feet tall.
I truly love her.

But now, I haven't seem Mimz in a while
But when I reminisce, I crack a smile.
I send a text to her now and then just to say,
Mimz, my true love for you is the same.

Natalie Williams (14)
Woodbridge High School

My Father

My father strolls across the golf course
Mapping exactly where he will put the ball next
Not too right, not too left
Firmly on the green

Unbelievable! He would hit the ball with ease
With his firm grip on the club
And the flow of the swing
The ball went too far for the eyes to see

He sometimes let me play
Taught me some of his techniques
I wasn't any good
But he still encouraged me

I wanted to be like my father
He inspired me in many ways
He was brilliant and successful
At everything he did

I was always getting in his way
Running, falling. But today,
It is my father who gets in the way of me
Yet, I admire him still.

Sam Everitt (14)
Woodbridge High School

Memories

Like an open book, you could read me;
You knew when things weren't right.
One time we sat up, crying and laughing,
As my worries disappeared into the night.

We eventually grew out of touch,
I watched our friendship slip away.
I didn't plan it to be like this
But my heart has gone astray.

I want it to feel like you've never been away,
Although it's been longer than I dare to say.
We've both got new friendships and new lives to lead
But can't you see through me? I'm empty, lost and alone.

I thought if I were to confide in you today,
You wouldn't believe a word I have to say.
I thought I'd have to get by once again on my own
With nothing but memories.

All the memories that I really need now,
I won't leave them behind;
They hold my life together - that will never change
I won't let them escape from my mind.

Georgia Green (14)
Woodbridge High School

My 'Follower' Poem

My grandfather worked in the fields,
His arms like tree trunks
Working in-between the corn furrows
The corn and canes ripped with one swipe.

A master. He would set the wing
Clutch his blade and prepare to swing.
The corn and sugar canes landed swiftly
Into the departure bags, to go out of the country.

His arm repeated swinging round and round
Until it was out of the ground. One eye
Narrowed at the ground with one finger raised
Tracking his path with his legs bruised and grazed.

I fell in the holes made by the missing plants,
Even getting muddy from the wet patched soil.
I sometimes got on his tractor and went all around the field
Bumping my head on the metal rod while I was kneeled.

I asked him if I would do the same,
To stand up tall and work all day.
All he ever did was follow. Until today when I realise
That he was only trying to be nice.

Keeping me out of trouble,
Hoping I would continue his work and give him a cuddle.
But until today I couldn't realise
That his words meant more to me than my life.

Amritpal Malhi (14)
Woodbridge High School

Cool School

Oh give me a school,
With a big swimming pool,
And students will think it's cool,

With diving boards and slides,
and a theme park with rides,
and geeks took the teacher's sides,

The teacher called Wayne,
Poor thing, went insane,
So we forced him on a plane to Spain.

All the teachers and geeks,
Were known as 'The Freaks',
So we put chewing gum on their seats.

So now the school is so cool,
Because we have the swimming pool,
And teacher's done nothing at all!

Nicola Thompson (13)
Woodbridge High School

Hurricane

H urricanes are wild
U nder the rain
R un and run
R ound the hurricanes
I ce is cold
C *rackle, snap, pop!*
A nd the hurricane stops
N earer and nearer
E nds right there.

Danni Bicette (11)
Woodbridge High School

My Sister And My Dog

I have a sister,
her name is Paige,
she doesn't like wearing the colour beige.

I have a dog,
he is small,
he is always playing with his colourful ball.

He likes to play,
with his bone,
he always has a plastic phone.

If he has been good,
we give him a treat,
if not, he will stamp his feet.

Luke Jones-Saunders (13)
Woodbridge High School

The Nine Eleven Bombings

The tragic day of 9/11
was the day many went to Heaven.
Lots of people, lots of regrets
but one thing's for sure, no one will forget.

The victims are miles from where we are
the friends and families are emotionally scarred.
Tons of people, tons of regrets
but one thing's for sure, no one will forget.

The emotional hurt, the physical pain
what did the bomber actually gain?
Many people, many regrets
but one thing's for sure, no one will forget.

Hundreds of lives were taken that day
the victims' families could only hope and pray.
Hundreds of people and also regrets
but one thing's for sure, no one will forget.

Lauren-Amber Morgan (13)
Woodbridge High School

River

A river can be longer than a mile,
A river can be in the shape of a smile.
A river can be a brilliant blue,
A river can be the colour of flu.

A river can be a home to a bird,
A river, a home that sounds absurd.
A river can be tiny and small,
A river can be big and tall.

A river can be a brilliant place,
A river has a lot of space.
A river can get bigger by rain,
A river getting bigger, that sounds insane.

Hayley Shannon (12)
Woodbridge High School

The Abyss

A gaping hole, mountains wide,
That sinks deeper than you could think.
Swimming down the diver sighed,
For uncharted waters he was in.

He heard a ripple, in the stone-dead space
So he turned around in fear,
And saw a flash in front of his face,
For uncharted waters he was in.

He steadied himself to rise
And straight from below it latched,
It took hold of his leg to his surprise,
For uncharted waters he was in.

It writhed and wriggled, not letting go,
So he unsheathed his knife,
And struck the fatal blow,
For uncharted waters he was in.

He let out a muffled cry,
What had he done?
So he said, 'Oh why, oh why?'
For uncharted waters he was in.

Deep down in the dark abyss
That sinks ever so deep
There is one more legend we will miss,
For uncharted waters the secret was in.

Alistair Bolt (12)
Woodbridge High School

Sunset

The sun slowly descends behind the clear blue veil of the sea.
The day star's beams flicker against the ocean's surface
as they gradually fade away.

A rainbow of colours dance among the tired fish.
Fiery tones of red, orange and yellow
battle against the cool, tranquil sea
as the clouds make a quick exit

Flocks of birds hush peacefully and fall asleep
to the lullaby of the wind.
In just hours the sun will rise again
but this is the time in which it leaves to light another realm.

Jasmin Johnson (12)
Woodbridge High School

A Day In The Life Of Me

The day starts early for me
The baby cries at six-thirty
My parents are blind
But I don't mind

I am only twelve and care for my brothers
Me and my sisters, we became like mothers
My parents are blind
But I don't mind

We can't use plates because we have no money
The children at school find it funny
My parents are blind
But I don't mind

Social Services won't help us
We can't even afford to get the bus
My parents are blind
But I don't mind

Sometimes I feel there is no way out
Then I really do start to doubt
My parents are blind and I really care
Sometimes my life just isn't fair.

Charlie Wade (13)
Woodbridge High School

Young Writers Information

We hope you have enjoyed reading this book - and that you will continue to enjoy it in the coming years.

If you like reading and writing poetry drop us a line, or give us a call, and we'll send you a free information pack.

Alternatively if you would like to order further copies of this book or any of our other titles, then please give us a call or log onto our website at www.youngwriters.co.uk

Young Writers Information
Remus House
Coltsfoot Drive
Peterborough
PE2 9JX
(01733) 890066